P9-DNY-304

A Remarkable Way to Achieve Your Dreams

FISH!™
FOR LiFE

Stephen C. Lundin, Ph.D.,
John Christensen, and Harry Paul

HYPERION

New York

Library of Congress Cataloging-in-Publication Data

Lundin, Stephen C.
    Fish! for life / Stephen C. Lundin, John Christensen, and Harry Paul.
      p. cm.
    ISBN 1-4013-0071-5
    1. Conduct of life. I. Christensen, John, 1959– II. Paul, Harry, 1950– III. Title.

BJ1597.L86 2004
650.1—dc22

                                    2003057030

Hyperion books are available for special promotions and premiums. For details contact Michael Rentas, Manager, Inventory and Premium Sales, Hyperion, 77 West 66th Street, 11th floor, New York, New York 10023, or call 212-456-0133.

FIRST EDITION

10 9 8 7 6 5 4 3 2 1

INTRODUCTION

When I was seventeen I began what I now consider to be "the six summers that shaped my life." For six consecutive summers I spent fourteen weeks working at Camp Courage.

Camp Courage, a camp for children with serious physical challenges, such as cerebral palsy and muscular dystrophy, was truly a magical place. The kids were given the opportunity to enjoy all the regular camp activities such as swimming, canoeing, overnights, and cookouts, only with the always-ready assistance of a few dozen teenage counselors. Parents benefited by getting a short break from caregiving and counselors were the unknowing recipients of valuable life lessons, lessons that sometimes lay dormant for years before revealing themselves. I was such a recipient and my lessons were many.

The culture of Camp Courage made a lasting and important impact on the way I view the world. It was the most upbeat, energetic, joyous, can-do, happy place I ever worked. It also had an element of radical authenticity and honesty that would bring to the surface all that was not real. Laziness and phoniness were exposed quickly by the intense, close-knit environment. At the time I was unaware of how rare such workplaces were.

We had a lot of fun at Camp Courage and the kids were fantastic. I remember seeing these children confront their physical limitations with attitudes that earned my lasting respect. They were my role models for expressing freedom in the face of limitations. Though they were limited physically, they made up for it by exhibiting the freedom to try just about anything. And they brought out the best in us. We wanted to make their summer special and we were aware that not all of the campers would live to return the next year.

It would be forty years before I labeled the Camp Courage way of being present in the world "the FISH! Philosophy." A chance event in Seattle was the catalyst. My colleague, John Christensen, needed to stay over a Saturday night in Seattle after we spent a week filming the poet David Whyte, who is known for taking his poetry into business organizations. John went shopping and happened upon a fish market that was so alive with positive energy that the documentary filmmaker in him just had to capture it. He produced a film about the market and we called it *FISH!* While the film was being edited, I wrote a book that we also called *FISH!* After that, the FISH! Philosophy was out of the tank.

Wherever you find the FISH! Philosophy, you will find the following ingredients (although the proportions may vary):

Play (fun and lightheartedness),

Make Their Day (a focus on engaging others in ways
   that lift their spirits),

Be There (living in the present moment and giving
   others our full attention), and

Choose Your Attitude (understanding that whatever
   attitude you are carrying with you right now, it is
   the one you are choosing).

The book *FISH!* was followed by the stories of real companies captured in *FISH! Tales.* Questions regarding how to keep the FISH! Philosophy alive for the long term are addressed in *FISH! Sticks.* And this book, *FISH! for Life*, is a result of something marvelous that happened as I traveled the world speaking about FISH! Those I met would often share their FISH! stories from the office and then add, often in conspiratorial whispers, "You know, this FISH! stuff works at home too!" And with only a little encouragement they would tell me their *personal* FISH! stories.

It became clear that at the end of the workday, lunch buckets and briefcases often carried something unusual home from the workplace. Nestled among the business documents, coffee thermoses, and leftovers was the FISH! Philosophy. *FISH! for Life* is a story of what can happen when FISH! goes home.

Stephen C. Lundin

Mary Jane and Lonnie

Four years had passed since Lonnie proposed to Mary Jane. They had been sitting in their favorite coffee shop, deep in the conversation of two people who woke up one day to find that a close friendship had become something romantic. Mary Jane had asked for some of the scone they typically shared 80/20, and when she looked down at what was pushed across the table it was not a scone at all. It was the large head of a monkfish with its mouth wide open. And in that massive open mouth was an engagement ring that, after a pause born out of shock, she gleefully accepted and allowed Lonnie to put on her finger.

Lonnie had access to an ample supply of fish heads from which to choose, as he was a well-known fishmonger at a famous Seattle fish market. Pike Place Fish was not only a fish market but also a tourist destination where people assembled each day in large crowds to watch the action and left with smiles and stories as well as fish. In fact, it was at the market that Lonnie and Mary Jane first met five years before, when she wandered in on her lunch break, attracted by the energy and carrying her brown bag lunch and a big problem. Lonnie, seeing the stress lines on her face, did what he does so well. He engaged her in a lighthearted conversation until the stress lines were erased by the natural smile lines underneath. He brought lightness to her countenance while he listened to her story.

1

Lonnie had no idea at the time of all the stress Mary Jane was feeling. He just responded to another human being, a human being who seemed to need a boost. Mary Jane had lost her husband and as a single mother of two, she had definitely needed the financial benefits of the promotion she had been offered. Even though she was aware of the terrible reputation of the group she would manage, she had accepted the position. She had hoped the problems in her new department had been exaggerated, but she soon realized they were actually worse than she could have imagined. She immediately encountered difficulties with her entrenched, entitled, and cynical staff. The day she walked into the market, she had no idea how to begin changing things and was deeply concerned and frightened.

As Mary Jane and Lonnie talked that day, Mary Jane described her promotion at First Guarantee Financial and the disgruntled and caustic staff she had inherited. Lonnie burst into laughter when she told him the managers at First Guarantee referred to her staff as "the toxic energy dump." Lonnie was impressed by her determination and curious about life in the big office buildings that overlooked the market.

Mary Jane wanted to know more about why the market was so full of energy and whether there were lessons to be learned from the market that could help her staff. Lonnie was delighted to be of service and not just because it was his nature; he also wanted to spend more time with her, being highly attracted from the first moment of their meeting. And so Lonnie agreed to explain the inner workings of the market at a later date.

Mary Jane was a good student and began to grow as a leader. Before long she had her staff coming to the market looking for ways to bring some of the energy to the third floor of First Guarantee, where their amazing accomplishments eventually became folklore.

Mary Jane and her team had discovered for themselves the old wisdom brought to life at the fish market, and they created on the third floor a workplace so attractive that there was a waiting list of applicants from other parts of the company. The work itself had not changed, but the way they chose to do their work each day had. As they evolved as a team, they created an appealing space where internal and external customers were served like they had never been served before.

But all of that was years ago. Mary Jane had since married Lonnie, been promoted again, and become swept up in the daily, hectic crush of life and work.

What Has Happened to My Life?

As Mary Jane Ramirez cleaned the house, she dusted around a small display of wedding photographs above the downstairs fireplace. She took a closer look at the pictures. The mix of fishmongers and First Guarantee employees outside the church always made her smile. She glanced out the window at the brilliant day and thought: *This is the kind of day you don't talk about with those who don't live here. If they knew we had days like this, they might move here and crowd the freeways even further.*

When she worked her way to the upstairs loft office, she could see the Space Needle, downtown skyscrapers, uptown high-rises, and the sparkling beauty of Puget Sound. Each of the windows in this room revealed a feast for the eyes, and the walls were covered with the most recent family photos. This had always been her favorite room: its contents reflected her new life with Lonnie. But this morning she noticed something—all of the pictures were from the first two years of their marriage. Where had the last two years gone?

A desk sat in front of each of the four Victorian windows. She remembered it was not uncommon in the early days of their marriage to find all four occupied in the evening. A typical night found Brad and Sarah, her children, as well as Lonnie, each with schoolwork or reading, and Mary Jane with the residue of daily work tasks. She strived during those first few years to protect her family time; and she was embarrassingly thankful for those evenings she could combine job and family by finishing up her First Guarantee work with her two children from her first marriage and her new husband busy around her.

Suddenly feeling anxious and a bit dizzy, Mary Jane sat down at her desk. The room and all the photographs had triggered something unsettling. *What happened to the dream that was to be my new life? I feel like I'm caught in a fast-*

flowing river of activity over which I have little control. What happened to the quiet intimate moments Lonnie and I enjoyed when we were dating and just married?

Mary Jane glanced down at her desktop. Sticking out from under the calendar was the edge of a sheet of paper that she recognized immediately in the way you would recognize an old friend. The words written on that piece of paper and the ones underneath had been a daily reminder during the most difficult time at work.

She looked at the wrinkled and coffee-stained paper. The words had started as notes from her visits to the fish market and evolved over many rewrites to become a precious guide for her work at First Guarantee. *So much has happened since that day I wandered into the fish market with a big problem and no solution.*

She pulled out the weathered pieces of paper and looked at them more closely. *It's time to recopy these, only this time I am going to enter them in my journal. I guess I have a bit of a paper and pen fetish*, she admitted to herself as she examined the neatly arranged contents of the bottom drawer. From underneath her colored pens she opened the box that contained her "special" journal paper and extracted a half-dozen crisp prepunched sheets of Levenger's finest. *A composer might use parchment*, she thought. *It is time these notes were treated in a manner consistent with their importance.*

Then, as she had done a half-dozen times before, she began to copy what had come to be called the FISH! Philosophy, revising and clarifying as she always did, based on her life experiences since the last rewrite. The words "natural energy" were written on a Post-it note and attached to the old version of the FISH! Philosophy. *Why did I put this here?* She put the note aside for the moment.

The FISH! Philosophy

The FISH! Philosophy is a way of life—based on old wisdom—that is easily viewed at the Pike Place Fish Market because it's on the surface there all day long every day. The twelve fishmongers who work in those twelve hundred square feet of energetic retail space embody the FISH! Philosophy. The wisdom there is like a rock outcropping that gives others a view of the deeper structure below the surface.

This old wisdom was not *created* by the market; it has been around almost since humans began to walk upright and converse. Rather, the FISH! Philosophy was *discovered* by this small group of fishmongers as they engaged in a process to achieve grace and excellence in their lives at work. They realized that playing around and having fun, making people's days brighter, being present, and choosing their attitudes consciously all contributed to a great workplace. The terms "Play," "Make Their Day," "Be There," and "Choose Your Attitude" became shorthand for their version of this old wisdom.

The four ingredients of the FISH! Philosophy were mixed in proportions unique to the market and fine-tuned until the staff's commitment to *being* world famous led them to *become* world famous. Now people arrive at the market from all over the world just to see this phenomenon firsthand; and most also go home with fish for the refrigerator, pictures for the scrapbook, and stories and memories for the heart.

Lonnie helped me discover the FISH! Philosophy and I helped my staff at First Guarantee do the same. Then my colleagues in other departments saw what we were doing, and that led to their own discoveries. Other companies also heard about our successes at First Guarantee and figured if it could be done at a financial institution it might be possible anywhere. At the very least, they were intrigued.

However, some of these organizations just wanted the results of FISH! without really committing to their own journey of discovery. They heard about the dramatic improvements at First Guarantee and wanted results of their own. And they wanted those results immediately.

Mary Jane thought, *Now I remember why I wrote that note to myself about natural energy.*

But many of these organizations that wanted instant results didn't want to change in any substantial way. This helped me understand that FISH! *only* works

with *"natural energy."* You can inspire colleagues to discover and practice the FISH! Philosophy but you can't
conscript or coerce them. You can model FISH!, but you
can't demand FISH! "Natural energy is the key to success when you need the full commitment of those
involved!"

Most of us have experienced quite enough "programs" in our lives. As a result, we shut down the
minute we think someone is trying to do something to
us or manipulate us rather than support us.

But while you can't *tell* people to FISH!, you can
model, expect, inspire, discuss, portray, and live FISH! It
may take a bit of patience, but most people want a better life for themselves and will join in once they know it
is authentic. Authentic journeys are fueled by *natural
energy*.

As she began to rewrite her notes on the first ingredient
of the FISH! Philosophy, Play, she happened to look over
at her color-coded calendar. *That's playful*, she thought.

Mary Jane had developed a color code so she could
see with one glance the balance of activities in the different facets of her life. It was a quick "life balance" indica-
tor. She used green ink for entries that related to work,
blue for community activities, yellow for family and marriage, orange for friends and self; Mary Jane looked down
at a sea of green with a sprinkling of blue coloring her
calendar.

Have I let quality time with Lonnie, the children, my

friends, and by myself get crowded out by the green and blue of life? Things have gone well at work, but now the rest of my life is out of whack. This is not what I imagined that day when I looked down at the open mouth of a fish and saw a ring. I love Lonnie and I love the way he has bonded with the children. But what has happened to the fun? When is the last time I went to the gym, spent time with friends, or read a book?

It was then she saw the one yellow inscription on the calendar, and it was placed on today's date. *Oh my goodness! Where has the time gone? I wanted to be at the market in time to help Lonnie celebrate his last day there.*

Lonnie's Last Day at the Fish Market

Mary Jane drove down Queen Anne Hill and parked near the market. She walked the four long blocks to Pike Place, and as she approached she heard the familiar sounds.

"One salmon flying away to Stockholm!" shouted Wolf as he launched a beautiful Copper River salmon toward the counter, to the absolute delight of the couple standing next to him. His customers had come all the way from Sweden to visit the World Famous Pike Place Fish Market and their faces were wet with tears of laughter.

"One salmon flying away to Stockholm!" the fish guys all chorused.

This place just gets better with age, thought Mary Jane as she walked into the market. *Now where is that man of mine?*

"Board in the sky," yelled one of the guys as he

returned a clipboard to the counter. "Board in the sky," echoed the others. A large group of children were grouped around the monkfish rigged to open and close its mouth. They were squealing with delight as a tall, hip-booted fishmonger affectionately named Insect worked his magic.

"Hey darling, what do you think of my garb?" It was Lonnie.

Mary Jane looked at her husband and audibly gasped. He was wearing a gold crown, made from a well-weathered shark jaw, and a garish purple velvet robe that had been decorated with strips of paper, each containing a phrase. She read some of the inscriptions:

This is my last day so let's party!
Play!
Make My Day
You can take the man out of the market but you can't
    take the market out of the man.
Gone fishing
One crab at a time, please
Have fun!
Want to see my shrimp?
Go fish!
Why not sing for the Halibut?

There were so many strips of paper attached to the robe that Lonnie looked a bit like a living crossword puzzle. His hip boots had also been written on by a number of unsteady hands as each of the guys had added their personal thoughts with a grease pencil.

"How are you doing, honey?"

"It is harder to say good-bye than I thought it would be," Lonnie replied. "I'm lucky that my last day is a busy day; no time to think about it."

"Well, just think of how excited you are to start school and how we have looked forward to having some time to ourselves again."

"That will be fantastic, won't it? Imagine me studying to be a nurse."

He bent down and gave her a quick peck, only to have Wolf shout out, "Hey, none of that lovey-dovey stuff." A slight blush formed on Mary Jane's cheeks. She smiled at the always-playful Wolf.

"I need to get back to work, sweetheart. Look at all these people. Who would have thought it?"

"They are here to say good-bye to you, Lonnie. The article in the *Seattle Times* about your retirement seems to have brought out many of your local customers."

The article described the fish market as a local treasure that had become an international tourist destination. On one Saturday alone a *Times* reporter had interviewed visitors from twenty-three different countries and asked each how they had heard about the market and why they had come. The answers made it clear that twelve hundred square feet of retail space in Pike Place was a magnet that drew people from all over the world. It didn't seem to matter where on the globe they resided; the fish market was on their lists of "Places I want to visit some day."

"I'll be across the street in the usual spot or I may run up to the office. I miss the kids, but it is nice to have some free time. Who knows, I might just journal a bit."

"Thanks, honey. Some of the guys are leaving early to decorate the party room at Takara. I can't really predict how long I will need to be here. It could be a few more hours before I can leave."

"I am looking forward to some time to sip a latte and do some journaling, so don't worry about a thing. Just enjoy."

"See you later." And with a final peck on the cheek, Lonnie was off to tend to a large family gathered around a grouper. Before he was through, he would make their day, be there, and sell them $243.00 worth of fish that would first fly to the counter and then to Oklahoma.

Mary Jane crossed the street to the coffee shop where Lonnie had taken her five years earlier when she brought her children with her to the market—the same coffee shop where he had later proposed. It was here that he had coached her on the four ingredients of FISH! She smiled as she remembered how Brad, who was just six at the time, had talked about his trip to the market and nothing else for weeks. *Lonnie has been so good for Brad. He really needed a man in his life and he took to Lonnie immediately.*

There may have been signs that something personal might develop between Mary Jane and Lonnie during those first encounters, but she was too engrossed with her problems at First Guarantee to notice.

She thought about her two children, now eleven and seven, and hoped they were having a good time with their grandparents in Los Angeles. Brad was four and Sarah was less than one when her husband, Ken, died. Ken's parents, a wonderful couple, had reached out to them and had stayed delightfully involved in their lives.

As she sipped her coffee, she struggled with the idea that it was Lonnie's last day at the market. In his twelve years there he had become an institution.

She thought about how Lonnie had dropped out of high school, but later, with help from Jack, the owner of Pike Place Fish, and the conscientious grandmother who raised Lonnie, he had earned his GED. That success gave him a much-needed boost in self-esteem and he then enrolled in Seattle Technical College. With Jack's financial and personal support, he persisted. Last year Lonnie finished the licensed practical nurse program going to school at night and doing his required internship on weekends. After receiving his LPN degree, he continued working at the market during the week and accepted an offer to continue weekends as an LPN at County General Hospital, where he had done his internship.

This was the first Saturday in months that Lonnie wasn't at County General at 6:30 in the morning. Instead, today he was at Pike Place at six in the morning, Mary Jane thought with a grim smile. *Well, that will change. I have been looking forward to the day when our lives can once again have the sense of nor-*

malcy that was lost when Lonnie started working on weekends. The choices we made—like my spending so many hours volunteering at the community center—all seemed so logical on paper, but the reality has sure put a strain on our life together. Well, hopefully that strain will end soon.

As she readjusted herself in the chair, she was confronted with an unwelcome thought. There had been less exercise and more comfort food in her life recently and the results were all too clear. *Fifteen pounds I didn't have three and a half years ago. How could I let that happen?* But Mary Jane knew how it had happened: One choice and one moment at a time, as the pressure of her demands crowded out what used to be a dedication to fitness; the loneliness of a life dominated by work and too many weekends home alone with children and no husband to provide personal breaks. It was just too much of an ordeal to get to the gym. Simply too much of a struggle to make good food choices.

I really need to do something about my weight and fitness and the way work seems to dominate my life.

An Unexpected Conversation with Wolf

"Earth to Mary Jane."

Mary Jane looked up at the market's biggest character, Wolf. "Hello, Wolf. I guess I was lost in thought. Sit down for a minute."

"This is a hard day for me, Mary Jane. I know that

what Lonnie is doing is good for him and I am happy for him, but I sure am going to miss the guy around here."

Mary Jane was a bit taken aback. She had never heard much in the way of feeling or sentiment from him. He was usually quite gruff, although everyone knew he had a heart of gold from his kind and generous actions. "That makes two of us, Wolf. I'm having a hard day as well."

Wolf sat down. Then Mary Jane remembered something Lonnie had told her. "Say, Wolf, Lonnie said you and your wife are adopting a child. How is that progressing?"

Wolf lit up like a Roman candle. "Oh Mary Jane, we just finalized the adoption two days ago. It's the best thing that ever happened to us. It is a miracle. Babies are amazing."

"Congratulations, Wolf. When you say it was a miracle, do you mean the odds of adopting are not good? I read that it has become quite difficult with some of the international developments."

"We are fortunate, but that's not what I'm talking about. We almost didn't make it as a couple."

"Excuse me, Wolf. I didn't mean to pry into your private life."

"That's cool, Mary Jane. Things are much better now and I don't mind talking to my best friend's wife about a happy ending. Say, I am hoping that you and Lonnie will be godparents for little Justin."

Mary Jane was stunned. This was more than Wolf had said to her at any one time since the day they had met at the market. And she had met Wolf's wife only briefly at a couple of parties; she remembered Roberta as a tall, striking woman who towered over Wolf by at least six inches. "Wolf, I am sure we would be delighted to be godparents, if that is what you and Roberta decide."

"We have already talked about it and we think you two are great examples of the values we want for Justin." He picked up on the sad look that passed over her face. "What is it, Mary Jane?"

"Oh, I've been thinking a lot about my life today. To be honest, I have been feeling a bit sorry for myself. I guess that happens sometimes when a busy life slows down enough to allow perspective. I know Lonnie and I are right for each other, but what difference does it make if we never see each other?"

"You two push it pretty hard, don't you? I know everything Lonnie has on his plate and I can only imagine how busy your life is now that you are famous and have a new promotion."

"I'm not famous, Wolf."

"Lonnie told me you were asked to speak to the Seattle Chamber of Commerce?"

"Yes, but that is no big deal."

"It is to me."

Mary Jane felt the need to change the subject and she was curious about something Wolf had said. "May I ask you a personal question, Wolf?"

"Sure."

"How did you turn things around?"

"The same way you turned things around at First Guarantee."

"But First Guarantee is a business. We are talking about a marriage."

Wolf just smiled.

"Did you take the ideas from the market home? You took the FISH! Philosophy home, didn't you, Wolf?"

Wolf just smiled again.

"And it helped, didn't it?"

Wolf smiled a third time.

"Will you tell me what you did? Please!"

Wolf shrugged in a slightly positive way.

"Please?" But before Wolf could respond, Mary Jane's cell phone began to ring.

"Excuse me, Wolf. Might be one of the kids."

Wolf smiled a knowing smile and gave a quick wave as he headed back to the market.

Caught in the Middle

Mary Jane answered the phone while quickly looking at the caller ID. "Hello, Mom." But it wasn't Mom.

"This is Officer Williams from the Seattle Police Department. I am sitting with your mother in front of the Sheraton Civic Center. She is quite disoriented and I don't think it would be a good idea if she drives her car. Could someone from the family come and pick her up?"

"Is she all right? Was there an accident?"

"She is fine and there wasn't an accident, but since she was driving on the wrong side of the street there could easily have been an accident if I hadn't pulled her over. She didn't remember your number but we found it programmed into her cell phone."

Mary Jane had a quick image of Sarah programming Grandma's cell phone a few weeks back and was silently thankful. "I'll take my own car home and be right down in a cab. May I speak with her?"

"Yes ma'am. And I really don't think your mother should be driving at any time."

"Mary Jane. Is that you?"

"Yes, Mom. I'll be right down."

"These streets are so confusing. I wish they wouldn't change things down here."

"We will talk about it later, Mom. I'll be right there."

Mary Jane raced to her car; she didn't even stop to tell Lonnie what had happened. Two hours later, she escorted her mom up the short flight of stairs to her mother's suburban apartment. Officer Williams had been pleasant and understanding, explaining that his own mother was the same age, but it was clear he thought her mother should no longer be driving. Mary Jane had to concur after she heard the whole story.

Mary Jane walked into the apartment with her. "Mom, I need to get back down to the market and I am going to use your car because mine is at home. After the policeman called me, I took a cab from home after dropping off my car. I need to use your car and later we need to talk about your driving."

"I wouldn't know what to do without my car, dear. I

use it for everything and other transportation isn't that convenient out here in the suburbs."

"I know, Mom. I'm sorry, but we want you safe. We love you. Let's talk some more later. I'll bet you are ready to put your feet up."

Her mother sank into her big chair and said, "When will you be bringing my car back?"

"I really don't think you should be driving, Mom. The officer was quite emphatic. We will talk about it soon, and in the meantime I will make sure you get to where you need to go."

"It wasn't my fault, dear. They changed the streets. How will I get groceries? How will I get to church? How will I get to photography club? What if you need me and I have to get over to your house quickly?"

"Trust me, Mom. We'll work it out, but I need to get back to the market. Did you know this was Lonnie's last day there?" Mary Jane gave her mother a quick recap in an attempt to take her mind off the car.

"That's nice, dear. I think I'll lie down for a minute."

"I'll call you later, Mom, and we can talk some more."

Back to the Market

Mary Jane returned to the market with a guilty feeling. She had just abandoned a needy parent. *What happened to all the parking spots? What will I do on Monday? Monday is the quarterly strategic planning meeting. I can't miss that. Where are all the parking spots?*

Mary Jane drove for blocks before finding a parking spot. It was now past peak time at the market but she could see it was still busy as she approached. None of the armless chairs near the fish stand were available so she once again wedged herself into a chair at the coffee shop. She glanced across the street but couldn't see Lonnie. *I hope he wasn't worried. Oh my goodness. I turned my cell phone off at the police station and forgot to turn it back on. She turned it back on, but there was no indication of any missed calls.*

Recognizing that she needed to calm down, she pulled out her journal and set it on the table in front of her. Opening her journal, she turned to the pages where she kept her favorite poems. Here she found a poem by David Whyte called "Sweet Darkness":

Sweet Darkness
BY DAVID WHYTE

When your eyes are tired
the world is tired also.

When your vision has gone
no part of the world can find you.

Time to go into the dark
where the night has eyes
to recognize its own.

There you can be sure
you are not beyond love.

The dark will be your womb
tonight.

The night will give you a horizon
further than you can see.

You must learn one thing.
The world was made to be free in.

Give up all the other worlds
except the one to which you belong.

Sometimes it takes darkness and the sweet
confinement of your aloneness
to learn

anything or anyone
that doesn't bring you alive

is too small for you.

Is my life too small for me? Have I made my life too small for me? I think what is happening with Lonnie and his career is positive, but then why aren't I happier and more alive?

Lonnie's New Life

Lonnie had been accepted by Washington State University College of Nursing in a special program. He would be able to complete the RN requirements and earn a BSN in three years while continuing to work part-time as an LPN—a lot of abbreviations to say the least. The Washington State program was designed to attract more men and women to the nursing profession at a time when it was hard to find enough registered nurses to staff the area's hospitals. Targeting married students with an interest in health care, but who could not afford to be totally jobless, it was perfect. A low-interest loan was part of the package.

But it meant that Lonnie had to leave the market. Mary Jane felt both pride in his accomplishments and sadness about his leaving the place where he had spent much of his adult life and some of his childhood. She knew Jack and the fish guys, and his deceased grandmother, were the only family he had ever known. *But now we are a family*, she thought.

Mary Jane looked over at the market and could see the first signs of cleanup as the crowd thinned and the fish guys began putting things away. She knew from experience that she had another half hour to herself—not enough time to go up to the office.

With more time to kill as the Saturday afternoon shadows lengthened, Mary Jane relaxed and let her mind wander. Across the street the playful and sometimes raucous noise from the market tapered off as the day drew to a close.

What am I going to do about Mom? She can't continue driving. She doesn't want to move into our extra room because she says she is afraid of losing her independence and thinks she will be too much of a burden on us, but without a car how much independence will she have? And she forgets important things like taking her blood pressure medicine.

And life is moving so fast. What about Lonnie? Is it realistic to think things will get better when he stops working on the weekends? What will we do to bring back the fun we had just living together?

Then she remembered her conversation with Wolf. It seemed like a long time ago, but she realized it was only a few hours. *I have always thought of FISH! as a work thing. But wisdom probably isn't bound to a location.*

Her attention was drawn to the street. Jack, the owner of the market, was walking toward her with Lonnie.

"Hi, Mary Jane. This has been quite a day and tonight should be a blast. But the Saturday after next should be even more interesting. You didn't tell Lonnie, did you?"

"Lonnie is clueless," Mary Jane responded with a smile and a bit too much enjoyment.

"Hey, wait a minute. It's not fair to gang up on me like this," said Lonnie.

"Mary Jane says you are available in two weeks and we have one more event planned to honor your retirement. We—" Jack actually giggled a bit here, then stopped to compose himself—"we are going to retire your apron!"

"You're going to what?"

"We are going to retire your apron, Lonnie. We have a

place on the back wall above the counter where we will hang it. Sort of like the football and baseball thing. You know, MJ, Dr. J, the two babes, and now Lonnie. It will be the first apron on the wall of fame for World Famous Pike Place Fishmongers. Who knows, you might get nominated to the Fishmongers Hall of Fame."

Lonnie was so tired all he could come up with was "Whatever."

"And Mary Jane, I think Lonnie has some good news to share. At least I hope it's good news. Well, I need to go home and pick up my wife. See you later."

The Volatile Drive Home

Lonnie and Mary Jane made the long walk to the back alley parking lot holding hands, looking in store windows, and talking about the day at the market. Lonnie had a burst of energy and wanted to share the conversations he had had with old customers. When they finally arrived at the car, Lonnie looked at it oddly and then got in without saying a word.

As they started down Fourth Avenue for the short drive to Queen Anne Hill, Lonnie blurted out, "We could have walked home in the time it took to get to the car." That was all it took for Mary Jane to burst into tears. She was crying so hard she had to pull over, as Lonnie sat completely confused by the outburst.

Although Lonnie had learned in his three years of

marriage that some things should not be rushed, they had only enough time left to change clothes and drive to Takara Restaurant if they wanted to be on time. And here they were sitting four blocks from home waiting for Mary Jane to stop crying. In the pressure of the moment, Lonnie said, "There is clearly something going on, Mary Jane, and I want to be there for you, sweetheart, but we have only thirty minutes before dinner."

Mary Jane turned stone cold as she looked at Lonnie and wiped her eyes. "You can go by yourself. There doesn't seem to be any time for me in your life anyway. Did you notice that I am driving my mom's car or were you so wrapped up in yourself that you didn't see that either? Do you ever think about me while you are running from one thing to another?" Each word had the hard edge of anger and Lonnie sat back in shock. Mary Jane pulled back into traffic and they rode the rest of the way in silence. As they pulled into the driveway, Lonnie had pulled himself together enough to simply say, "I'm sorry."

Mary Jane sat staring ahead for a long moment and then turned to Lonnie. "I know I have been busy also, too busy to even notice how frustrated I had become with our life.

"But this is your big day and I don't want to completely ruin it for you. My stress isn't a result of what happened today; it just surfaced today. Let's go to the party and try to have a good time if we can."

"You mean the world to me, Mary Jane. And I think of Brad and Sarah as my children now, even though I know they will always have a connection to their real dad that I can't replace. Can we at least talk on the way to the party? I really do want to know what's happened and why you are driving your mom's car."

And so they changed clothes and on the way to the party she described the facts of her day, avoiding her concerns about an expanding waistline and everything else that was troubling her. She simply focused on the dilemma with her mom.

On arriving at the party, they allowed themselves to quickly get caught up in the festivities.

Brad and Sarah Return

Lonnie and Mary Jane stood together by the Alaska Airlines gate as the passengers from Los Angeles disembarked. Watching the diversity of people from LA is usually entertaining, but after a late night and an early morning they were a bit numb and drowsy as they waited for the kids. Because Brad and Sarah were unaccompanied minors, UAMs as they are called by the airline personnel, Lonnie and Mary Jane were allowed to come all the way to the gate on the other side of the security stop. They could hear Brad and Sarah before they could see them.

"And we rode on Space Mountain two times and I closed my eyes and raised my hands and it was so cool . . . Mom! Lonnie!"

An amused flight attendant handed the children over,

along with the paperwork, as she worked around the perimeter of an all-family hug.

The ride home was full of stories about the trip to LA until Brad, always the intuitive sort, spoke up sharply. "Is everything all right?"

Mary Jane decided to limit her response. "Grandma had some difficulties while you were gone."

"Is she all right, I mean safe and everything?"

"Yes, Brad, she is fine and is looking forward to seeing you two."

"Why are we driving her car?"

"Well, she had a problem driving the wrong way on a one-way street and I decided it would be better if she didn't have access to her car. In fact, I don't think she should be driving at all anymore."

Brad thought about that for a while and said, "But she does so much stuff. How will she get around?"

"We haven't worked out the details yet. This just happened yesterday. But Lonnie and I want you and Sarah to be a part of the discussion about Grandma. Some of the possible solutions will affect you."

"You mean Sarah and I get to talk about adult stuff? Wow."

Mary Jane and Lonnie exchanged smiles. And then Mary Jane remembered that her darling boy's difficulties at school still had not been resolved. A few days ago, his teacher had told her Brad had become increasingly moody in class. She put the thought aside. *I can't solve it now.*

"Lonnie and I need to call an adult time-out while you two unpack. Do you remember about adult time-outs?"

"Yes, Mom."

"But before we go home I have a surprise."

"I know," said Sarah. "We are going to see Grandma."

"Yes, we are. How did you guess that surprise so easily?"

"Aren't we driving toward her house?"

Lonnie added, "Your sense of direction is so good I think you should drive, Sarah."

Sarah was still giggling when they arrived to take Grandma to brunch.

A Serious Conversation

Lonnie and Mary Jane met that evening in the shared office space upstairs while the kids finished unpacking. After a brunch with their often-confused grandma, Brad and Sarah had a better idea of the dilemma. As they pulled their chairs together, the gravity of their discussion was weighing heavily on both of them.

Mary Jane looked directly at Lonnie. "I am not sure my mom should be alone. She seems to have trouble remembering the everyday important things and I worry about her remembering to take her medications. I hadn't noticed that before yesterday, had you?"

"Not to the extent we saw today. It worries me too. I have heard of something called small strokes. And I have seen people in the hospital with similar symptoms. Her confusion may be a sign that she has had some ministrokes and didn't even know it. Sometimes the confusion is only temporary. A doctor's appointment is definitely a priority."

"Definitely! Lonnie, help me think this through. She shouldn't drive. Agreed?"

"She was asking about her car at brunch and when we will be bringing it back, but yes, I agree."

"And she has made it clear she doesn't want to bother us by moving. Do you think that will change? A nursing home or assisted living center seems like such a dramatic change."

"I am not an expert on this, Mary Jane, but sometimes the elderly emphasize not being a burden. It doesn't necessarily mean that she would refuse to move in with us. She may simply be trying to respect our life."

"But what about you, Lonnie? Would you want my mom in the house 24/7?"

"It would be a big change, Mary Jane, but when your mom drove the wrong way on a one-way street, all of our lives changed. It's going to take a lot of juggling and planning to do what we need to do for her, regardless of where she lives. If she stays in her apartment, the distance between her apartment and our home is an inconvenience."

Lonnie looked at Mary Jane thoughtfully, then said, "I have heard about adult communities where they have a full range of services for seniors. The hospital runs a community like that called Forest Glen. The pictures show a rural setting with lots of trees and I think it is actually closer than her apartment and doesn't require crossing town."

"And there is home care and meals on wheels," added Mary Jane. "She could move closer and have that kind of support."

"But what do you want, Mary Jane?"

"I think what I want is too much to ask of you and I don't know if Mom would agree anyway."

"I need to tell you something important, Mary Jane. My grandma went into a nursing home and I remember feeling so guilty about not being able to do more, but as a single guy I just couldn't see taking on the responsibility. You see, it has been a tradition in my culture to bring the elderly into the family home and it seems like the right thing to do. I want your mom here if you do. I think it would be the right thing for us to do and a great life experience for the kids."

"Oh, Lonnie." Mary Jane swallowed a couple of times but couldn't continue, so she simply got up and gave Lonnie a hug. Finally she was able to finish what she was saying. "That is so generous, sweetheart. Do you think it's time to get the kids involved in this discussion?"

"Absolutely!"

The Family Council

Shortly after they invited the children upstairs, Brad surprised them all by saying, "I think she just needs to know we really, really want her to live with us. So do we really want her to live with us? I do. That would be cool having Grandma in the house."

"Brad. That is so kind and generous of you."

Brad looked at Mary Jane with a proud set to his face. "Thanks, Mom. I love Grandma."

"Me too," said Sarah. "And she can sleep with me."

Sarah's innocent comment evoked big grins all around and some emotion in Mary Jane. "I think she might prefer the guest room because it has a bathroom so close, but you are also kind, Sarah. We certainly have the room in this big old place and Mom is quite capable of making a contribution to the household chores and to the budget. We have one big challenge, though."

"What is that, Mom?"

"Brad said it. We need her to know we really want her so she doesn't say no just because she fears being a burden. She has every right to choose her own life, but we don't want her to say no for the wrong reason."

Lonnie added, "And if she chooses to move in, our lives will be different for some time to come. For a while she will continue being our best babysitter, but eventually she may require some help herself, like my grandmother did when she broke her hip."

This comment by Lonnie led to a discussion with the children about his life before they knew him and he shared the tradition of many different cultures of welcoming the elderly in their children's homes. This caused the ever-thoughtful Brad to question how he and Sarah would decide who got to invite Lonnie and Mary Jane into their home when they grew up.

Mary Jane felt both relief and fear as the decision became clear and the weight of that decision obvious. She blurted out, "It will be like putting fuel on the fire for us. Our lives are already full to the brim. So much so that . . ." She stopped as she realized the children were present and it might not be the best time to expose her and Lonnie's personal problems. She quickly recovered by saying, "I think she will accept our invitation if we convince her we are serious. Brad is right; she needs to know we really want her. Well, I am not sure exactly how to approach this issue with Grandma, but it's bedtime for all those going to school tomorrow."

After the kids were settled, Lonnie looked at Mary Jane and said, "Big day, huh?"

"Big day and big weekend. Oddly enough, I am feeling really hopeful right now even though I am overwhelmed by the thought of Mom moving in with us. Are you headed for bed?"

"I am. Are you coming?"

"Not quite yet, sweetheart, but I know your morning is earlier than mine. I have one phone call to make."

One Phone Call and Then to Bed

Mary Jane returned to the upstairs office, where she had started the crazy weekend dusting and rewriting her notes. She found the phone number for which she was looking. Glancing at her watch, she thought, *I wonder if 9:45 is too late to call Janell on a Sunday night. I don't think so. She has two little ones and likes the quiet of the evenings to wind down with her husband, Jimmy.*

Janell Wong had become Mary Jane's closest friend at work. Janell was the first of her employees to see the possibilities in FISH! and quickly became an ally in the turn-around of the third floor. Already a well-liked supervisor, she demonstrated remarkable leadership ability, and others in the organization began recruiting her. Janell was committed to the third floor, but Mary Jane encouraged her to consider the offers. A year ago Janell accepted a promotion to head up the customer service center, and they talked regularly about work and life. Mary Jane dialed Janell's number.

"Hello, Jimmy. Is it too late to talk with Janell? Thanks.

"Hi, Janell. Are the kids tucked away?"

"They are sound asleep, Mary Jane. Is everything all right? This is late for you."

"The honest answer is yes and no. Do you have time to join me for lunch next week? I would like your help on something. Wolf and I are going to meet at the market and I would like you to be there."

"That would be like old times. Just tell me where and when."

"I'll let you know when I set it up. Any days better than others?"

"I'm open all week except for Monday."

"Thanks, Janell. I'll let you get back to your family. I really appreciate this."

"No problem. Are you going to keep me in the dark until then?"

"Well, you told me once that you got some ideas from FISH! that helped you become a better mom. I would like you to bring those ideas."

"Will do. That's the easiest assignment I have had in a while. See you next week. Bye."

"*Ciao.*"

Back to the Wolf Den

Mary Jane and Janell arrived at the market with their brown bag lunches on Wednesday. Mary Jane caught Wolf's attention and then headed across the street, where she and Janell arranged three chairs around a table vacant only because its chairs were scattered all over the patio.

Mary Jane had been through this drill before. On a sunny day the place was always packed at lunchtime. They ordered a soft drink for Wolf and cappuccinos for themselves. Mary Jane started to sit down in an armless chair and then thought better of it, leaving it for the two-hundred-plus-pound Wolf. Janell saw this and commented.

"What's the deal with the musical chairs?"

"Oh, this is just a dance I created to celebrate a few unwanted pounds."

"Cute. There is a lot of that going around. And around. And around."

"Come on now, Janell; your weight hasn't changed an ounce in all the time I have known you except during pregnancy."

"I am not sure that's true, but I do have a strategy. I eat often with fish."

"You eat a lot of fish?"

"No. I eat often with FISH!"

Mary Jane still missed the point. "I can't wait to hear about that, but it will have to wait. Here comes Wolf."

"How are you lovely young ladies today? Janell, right?"

"Yes it is, Wolf."

"As I mentioned on the phone, Wolf, I think Janell may have something to add to our discussion. Call it female intuition."

"Well, I'm in favor of anything female. Right now the guys are dying to know what I am doing over here with you two attractive women. Of course, they recognize you, Mary Jane, but Janell will keep their imaginations occupied. Tell me again what is on your mind."

"It was the way you just smiled the other day when we were talking and I asked you if you took the FISH! Philosophy home. You did, didn't you?"

Wolf smiled.

"Come on, Wolf. Did I read too much into your encouraging shrug when I asked if you would help me?"

"I'm a pretty private person and you got me talking

about things I don't usually talk about. But I want to be of help if I can. First tell me what the big deal is."

"Fair enough. I have a son who is starting to act up at school and is often moody at home. I have a wonderful husband I hardly see because of our mutually exclusive work schedules. My mother is having some problems and may be moving in with us. And I have added many pounds of unwanted adipose tissue in the last three years; and that is without really trying. Quite simply, my home life stinks right now—even though on the outside it might look like I have everything." At this point a startled Janell reached over and put her hand briefly on top of Mary Jane's.

"Is that about it, Mary Jane?" said a thoughtful and smiling Wolf.

"No! Since you asked, I have been snipping at people who take too long to get my order at the store; I'm often grumpy and grouchy at home; and when I sit down to think about what has happened to me—something I never have time to do—I realize I am not really enjoying my life. I even sank so low as to get short with my mother about something over which she had no control."

"OK. Is that about it?"

"Yes! Isn't that enough?"

"I can give you more time if you need it," said the grinning Wolf.

"Why are you still smiling? This is serious, Wolf. I don't like me."

"Settle down. I'll tell you why I'm smiling. I'm smiling because here you are—the woman who transformed an organization from what was called a toxic energy dump into a productive and enthusiastic place to work by discovering for yourself the same ingredients that make up our culture at the market. And yet you haven't made a very basic connection to your life.

"You have everything you need, Mary Jane. You know all you need to know. The FISH! Philosophy is not just a work philosophy, although you and I have applied it to work with great results. The FISH! Philosophy is a philosophy of life. Life at work or life at home—it's all life, Mary Jane. Both can benefit from a little more fun, a selfless approach, being present for others, and a careful consideration of the attitude we are choosing.

"And there was another reason I was smiling. I was slow to make the connection myself, yet I believe these ingredients probably saved my marriage when I finally took them home. There you have it. How about you, Janell?"

"Can you say a bit more about that, Wolf? Your marriage, I mean."

Wolf took a deep breath and just sat for a moment. "This is hard for me. OK. The divorce papers were actually being drafted and I asked myself if I had done everything I could. I had this insight that the things I had tried to do to save my marriage always involved my wife and usually backfired. So I began to consider things I could do on my own. This may sound a bit crass, but I realized that my wife was more important to me than all of my customers at the market and that I really didn't want a divorce. So I began treating her as if she were more important than any customer who ever came into the market. I would do little things for her. I would try to be lighthearted when she was around. When she said something I would listen intently, and I began monitoring my attitude at home.

"After two weeks, she started to look at me differently. One day she said something had changed but she wasn't sure what. Then I noticed she started to respond in kind. One morning I found a little heart in the bathroom with a simple note written on it, and things have been getting better ever since."

Mary Jane was stunned and sat with her mouth open. Then she said, "I am sorry, Wolf. I never even knew you were having problems until you alluded to it the other day. Thanks."

Janell said, "That makes it easier for me, Wolf. Thank you." Wolf nodded.

Janell continued. "I have two children with learning disabilities and found myself dreading the end of the work day. I love those kids, but the more I tried to control them the more difficult it became. One day I figured I had nothing to lose, so I took FISH! home. The whole dynamic of my relationship with the kids has changed. They will always have their special challenges, but we have discovered a way to be together that is a lot more satisfying for them and for me.

"My neighbors probably think I am crazy, but we dance with the vacuum cleaner. We sing when we're doing the dishes. And we have created a dozen ways to have fun with schoolwork.

"I made up this Scandinavian accent I use to tell them things that they used to reject. And best of all, we can go out to dinner now. Our game is to see who can make the waitperson's day.

"When we talk, I sit down next to them rather than try and juggle the conversation with whatever else I am doing. We make a game of surprising each other with little gifts and gestures and always tell one another when the other person makes our day.

"And I found a sticker book with all kinds of different faces—happy, sad, angry, surprised, and a hundred others. Do you know what I am talking about?" Mary Jane and Wolf nodded and Janell went on.

"I will call an attitude break and we all sit down and put a sticker in our calendar to most closely match our attitudes. Then we talk about the choices we made and discuss any new attitudes we are going to try. At the very least we are now conscious of our attitudes and skillful at naming them. I don't think we will need the stickers much longer and will be able to shift to words instead."

Mary Jane was writing everything in her journal. She looked at her two tablemates and said, "All right, thanks. That's great, Janell, but I could really use some more ideas here. How about some more specifics? Tell me how to do this."

Wolf and Janell just smiled.

"Really. I want some more specifics I can take home and use. It sounds like you guys must have hundreds of ideas."

Wolf and Janell just smiled.

"What?"

Janell came to her friend's rescue. "Mary Jane, I will never forget the day you came back from the market so full of energy. You wanted so badly to make some immediate changes, but instead what did you do?"

"Well, I was afraid if I came on too strong, you would think it was a fad or program or something and back off. So I looked for a way to help you make the same discovery that I had made. I knew the energy had to be natural, and if I put on a lot of pressure you might go along for a while but it wouldn't last."

"And what are you asking us to do now?"

"I get it. So you guys are gently telling me something I should already know from my own experience. I can't take your ideas and implement them. I have to join my family in a discovery process of our own."

"Don't be too hard on yourself. It's when you are stressed or under pressure that it is most difficult to see the obvious. Much of the power, as you know, is in the discovery."

"OK. But I would find it both helpful and provocative to hear your stories."

Wolf and Janell nodded and they spent the rest of their time together sharing more of their stories. Not so Mary Jane could copy the ideas and implement them, but so she could be inspired by them to discover her own path.

When they were finished, Mary Jane thanked them and said, "So now it is up to me. I mean us."

Wolf and Janell just smiled, and Mary Jane laughed.

Then Wolf hit her with another thought that was so obvious as to be easily missed. "Don't forget you have the world's foremost experts in your own home."

"It hasn't escaped my attention. What is it they say about the cobbler's children not having any shoes? But as much as we know FISH! at work, I think we are in the elementary stages on a path of discovery at home."

The Hall of FISH! Fame Ceremony

Mary Jane had never seen the market this busy. It was hard to move, but the guys seemed to find a way to keep selling fish and engaging the crowd. Wolf and JD were showing off. When Wolf received an order for two fish, he threw them to JD at the same time and JD caught them both. The crowd went nuts. If they only knew how long Wolf and JD had practiced—using two greased rubber fish. But it all paid off today, as they made memories for all of the customers.

A red-faced administrator from the marketplace was frantically trying to clear an aisle. As he did this, he managed to irritate everyone he encountered. *Boy, is he out of place here*, thought Mary Jane. *He should go back to his office until the fun dies down.*

Jack took the microphone that sat on the counter. Lonnie was standing next to him. Jack turned on the mike and it made the customary screech that had everyone covering their ears. After a few adjustments, he was ready.

"Today is a special day for Pike Place Fish. It is a sad day as one of our best is leaving. It is a happy day because he is pursuing an educational degree that will allow him to have the career of his dreams in a healing profession. For thirteen years Lonnie has been a leader at Pike Place Fish and we will greatly miss him. He was one of the brash young men who first said, 'Why not be world famous?' We owe him a great deal.

"Today, for the first time, we at the World Famous Pike Place Fish Market will retire an apron. As we do that, we at the same time establish our hall of fame. Well, actually, it isn't a hall, just that beam over there."

There were a few chuckles and Jack took the apron from Lonnie, got up on a stool, and nailed it to the beam above the counter. There was thunderous applause and someone shouted, "Speech, speech." Soon the entire crowd was chanting, "Speech."

Lonnie held up his hands for silence as he took the microphone. "Thank you, Jack. Thirteen years ago you gave a wild kid a chance by offering him a job, a caring adult role model, and a place to hang out. That kid was heading in the wrong direction, already in trouble with the law. The foster mom who was trying so hard to raise him just had too many troubles of her own. You didn't hesitate to take this kid under your wing and to teach him to work, to get along, to grow up, and to value education. Jack, sometimes I think I owe you my very life."

Lonnie's voice was cracking and tears were streaming down his face. He paused for a moment and then continued: "In the time I have been here, I have watched you do the same with a number of young men. I think you are a community treasure and I love you. Thanks from me and all the other guys you have helped along their paths."

Mary Jane was churning with emotion herself as she looked up at her husband and then over at Jack. Jack had a handkerchief in his hand and was pretending to wipe his nose as he wiped his eyes.

Lonnie paused a second time to compose himself. Many of the fish guys were doing the same thing. Some of them were obviously the young men to whom Lonnie referred.

"And these guys, what can I say? They are a mess!" He waited for the laughter to stop. "No, really, they are great. These guys are my brothers. We supported each other in our work and in our private lives. We created a world famous fish market that others look to as an example. I'm going to lose it if I don't stop here. Thanks, Jack. Thanks, guys. Thanks, Mary Jane. And thanks to all of you who have honored me with your business over the years." He raised his fist in the air and shouted, "Keep eating fish!"

The applause continued for a long time. Jack, always the entrepreneur, took the microphone and announced a special: "For the next hour, any fish purchased will be thrown to Lonnie by the salesperson. Or, if you so choose, you may throw the fish yourself! If he misses, the fish is free. Later Lonnie will sign your World Famous Pike Place Fish Market T-shirts and hats."

It was pure bedlam. Everyone in the crowd seemed to

want to throw a fish. After an hour, the sales total was enormous, but there had been no free fish. After all, Lonnie was a pro when it came to catching fish. The line for T-shirts and hats to be signed later stretched all the way to First Avenue.

Mary Jane decided this would be a good time to prepare for the second family council meeting that would take place Sunday night. Her trusty all-purpose journal was in her tote bag, and she headed for the coffee shop a block away.

A Surprise Meeting with Janell

As Mary Jane wove her way through the crowd and down the street, she became aware that someone was a half step behind her. She looked back to see Janell working hard to catch up. She reached Mary Jane just as they approached the entrance of the coffee house.

Mary Jane stepped back and out of the way so a tour group could take their picture in front of Starbucks and then gave Janell a big hug. "I didn't see you until a second ago, Janell."

"Like you could see anyone in that crowd. It was a touching ceremony, don't you think?"

"Very emotional. I think Lonnie is ready for a change, though. And I will enjoy holding hands with a man who doesn't have the cuts and slices that go with catching flying fish. Is this a coincidence that we arrive here at the same time?"

"I thought you might enjoy some company. You know, someone to bounce things off of. As we talked yesterday, I thought about how grateful I am for all you have done for me. You saw something in me I didn't even see in myself and my life has been better ever since. So I want to be there for you.

"I'll bet you have your journal in that bag and you are planning to do some writing over coffee. If you would rather be alone, just tell me."

"You are a sweetheart and you know me too well. Let's get some coffee and find a place to sit down. The journal can wait."

Since Starbucks had no place to sit they took their skinny lattes (light on the foam, please, extra shot, extra hot) across the street to see if they could find a bench in the park. The park was surprisingly empty and they found a bench in the sun and overlooking the waterfront.

"Want to talk about the things you wouldn't say in front of Lonnie's best friend?"

"You picked up on that, did you? Yes. I think it would be helpful to say some of what is on my mind out loud. With all that is going on, it's like Lonnie and I share a home but not a life. We got married because we loved being with each other and now we hardly see each other. Janell, I just want a little more joy in my life. Am I being selfish?"

"Don't you think every young married couple goes through this adjustment period? One or two careers, kids, church, outside interests, aging parents, exercise, education, and all the rest of life add up to quite a full plate."

"Thanks, Janell, but I don't consider us a young married couple. We have a young marriage, that is true, but we are not kids. And I wish you hadn't mentioned exercise. Exercise dropped off of my schedule months ago. There just wasn't time for everything. And when it dropped by the wayside, a number of other things dropped as well."

Janell chuckled at that. "Yes, you mentioned that the other day."

"Come on, Janell, you could be a fashion model. You must eat nothing but carrots."

"Like I said, I would be happy to tell you what it takes to keep things from expanding and dropping any time you wish. I think you will find my approach familiar. But right now what I want to be sure I understand is what's making you so unhappy. Yes, you are busy, but you have some great things happening in your life."

"Let me explain with a story. When I lost Ken so suddenly and found myself alone with two young children at the same time that I was experiencing an unstable work situation at First Guarantee, I became vividly aware of how things can turn on a dime. I made a commitment to live my life to the fullest. I like to think of that as a gift of perspective left me by my first husband.

"But my life has accelerated and I am losing that perspective. In fact, I'm no longer sure what it means to be living my life to the fullest. Does living life fully mean doing a lot of stuff or really being present for the most important things?

"Sometimes it seems like I am just passing through

much of my life at home, and I feel like Lonnie and I have let things take the course of least resistance without ever asking what we really want. I'm not sure what to do. Everything we have on our plate seems important."

"Have you and Lonnie talked about this?"

"Well, I had a bit of a breakdown the night of his party and I felt bad later. We made a pact to talk more but haven't had time yet. There never seems to be a free moment to just talk anymore."

"When life is overwhelming, it is often helpful for me to choose one thing and give it my attention. Is there something that needs attention now?"

"Mom. How am I going to respect her independence and still face the fact that she is no longer able to drive and may not always remember to take her medications?"

"What do you intend to do now?"

"I would really like her to move in with us. That would be my wish. And I need to let her know in a compelling way that she is wanted, while still respecting her right to control her life. We are going to have a second family council about Grandma and I could use an idea or two."

"I think this would be a great subject to approach using the FISH! Philosophy."

Mary Jane looked at her friend and smiled. "Aren't you the best friend in the world? The idea was too close to see. That is what we will do. We will use the FISH! Philosophy to guide our discussion. The kids will be able to be full participants that way."

"That sounds like a neat idea, Mary Jane. I'm going to

let you get back to your journal now. I have a few things left to do today."

"You were sweet to find me, Janell, and you have been soooo helpful. Say hello to Jimmy. Bye."

Entries in the Journal

Mary Jane walked across the street for more coffee, and when she returned to the park her bench was occupied. So she ended up sitting on the ledge that surrounded the fountain.

She opened her journal and created a new heading and underlined it. Then she added some bullet points underneath. Sitting back, she thought about what she had put down.

FISH! FOR LIFE

- *Grandma*
- *Marriage*
- *Raising children*
- *Friends*
- *Weight loss*

Closing her eyes for a minute, she found herself looking at the kaleidoscope of colors and shapes created by the sun shining intensely on her eyelids. *What now*, she thought.

She opened her eyes and turned to the part of her journal where she accumulated wisdom and inspirational quotes. And there were the first lines of a Mary Oliver poem titled "The Journey." They were words that carried a lifetime worth of wisdom:

> One day you finally knew
> what you had to do, and began.

Those lines say it all. "One day you finally knew/what you had to do, and began." And began . . . Well, I know what I need to do. It's time to begin.

Second Family Council

The family had assembled in the upstairs office and all four desk chairs were occupied. Mary Jane looked at the children and said, "Let's talk about FISH! I think the FISH! Philosophy might be useful in thinking of ways to welcome Grandma and make her comfortable here."

"Cool. That's the stuff you and Lonnie use at work, right?"

"It is, Brad. Lonnie schooled me on FISH! and I took it to work. I remember well your first visit to the market. Do you?"

"Yeah, I helped Lonnie with his work. We had fun."

"I remember too," added Sarah. "A fish bit me."

"It did not."

"Did too."

"Did not."

"All right, kids. Sarah, I don't think it bit you. I think you were startled when its mouth moved."

"That's what I meant, Mom."

"Are we going to throw fish to Grandma?"

"Why don't Lonnie and I go through the four parts of FISH!, and we can all discuss how to welcome Grandma."

🐟 PLAY 🐟

"How can we make this fun? Play is the first ingredient of the FISH! Philosophy. It means being lighthearted, playful, and fun. It is a way to make the ordinary and routine more interesting and engaging by having fun with whatever you are doing."

Play: Carry a light heart with you wherever you go.

In the beginning of a FISH! journey, play may be as simple as adding some fun to the daily routine. After a while you learn that the playful energy engendered by special events can be chosen as an attitude at any time. Ask yourself:

- How might I be an instrument of lightheart-edness?
- Do I have a smile in my heart that is heard in my voice?
- Do I explore all the ways I could bring fun to a task that is not usually fun?
- Am I choosing playfulness?

"Mom."

"What, Sarah?"

"What is a 'losophy'?"

"That is a big word, isn't it? It is pronounced phil-os-o-phy."

"Philosophy?"

"Yes, and the FISH! Philosophy is a way of approaching life. So let's pretend you are doing something you would rather not be doing."

"Like doing the dishes or cleaning my room?"

"Right. Remember the time the dishwasher was broken and we were doing the dishes together and making up puzzles and trying to stump each other?"

"Yes. That was fun!"

"Did we get the dishes washed?"

"They were really clean because we didn't want to stop washing."

"We took a chore you don't enjoy naturally and made

it fun by the way we did it. That's the FISH! Philosophy in action. And the first part of the philosophy is Play. So the question is, how can we make welcoming Grandma to our house fun and playful? Grandma will be giving up her independence and may have some doubts and fears. How are we going to make welcoming Grandma fun?"

"Do you mean when I play with my dolls it's a philosophy? I play all the time, Mom. Don't all kids play?"

"Yes. It means play is an important part of your life. Sometimes adults forget to play. Kids know how to play."

"How can we play?"

"Grandma can play with my dolls anytime," offered Sarah.

"Do you think Grandma would want to play catch?"

"I'm not sure, Brad, but she would love to be invited."

"I know she likes to play cards too. We play Kings in the Corner all the time."

"Great. What are some other things we could do to make her move here fun?"

"We could play Hide-and-Seek," suggested Sarah.

"Oh sure," added her big brother. "Why not Pin the Tail on the Donkey?"

Lonnie said, "Let's play with Sarah's idea for a minute. I have a hide-and-seek idea. We all seem to think that Grandma just needs to know we really want her in our home. That if we convince her our wish that she join us is real, she will agree to move in with us. But we don't know that for sure and need to be sensitive to her need to control her own life. How could we make the idea of moving here a fun surprise and still respect Grandma's right to be in control of her life?"

"She loves the zoo," said Sarah. "I know because she takes me there all the time. We could tell her we are taking her to the zoo and bring her here."

"And we could have some of her things ready for her to move in, arranged just the way she likes them," added Mary Jane. "We just need to let her know we are more than willing to move her things back to her apartment if need be. It could be a demonstration of our commitment to the idea of having her move in."

"And we could have balloons and her favorite meal," suggested Brad.

Lonnie was looking at the ceiling and thinking. "One of us is going to have to drive her wherever she goes now. How often does she go to the hairdresser?"

Mary Jane thought for a minute. "Not that often and it's irregular. She doesn't like spending money on herself."

Lonnie said, "Well?"

MAKE THEIR DAY

Mary Jane looked baffled, but Brad had picked up on the idea and spoke. "We can give her a hair thing."

Lonnie smiled. "I don't know what it is called either, Brad. A 'hair thing' will have to do for now. The second part of the FISH! Philosophy is Make Their Day, which means making life brighter for people by doing special things or doing things in special ways. How could we make a hair thing really special?"

Mary Jane looked at Lonnie and Brad, who were both grinning. "It's called a permanent and we could take her to a spa where she could have a permanent and also get pampered."

"That we could, darling. And while she was there, we could move some of her things into the guest room. Then we think of some reason to stop by here, rather than taking her back to the apartment. We will surprise her with a big welcome and the furnishings will demonstrate we really want her to stay."

"Not too many of her things, though. I think there might be a fine line between feeling wanted and feeling trapped."

"Good point. Perhaps just something symbolic, perhaps her favorite ottoman."

"Yes!" said Mary Jane with new animation in her voice. "Just one piece of furniture should make the point without overdoing it. So we surprise her with a gift of a spa treatment and then we surprise her again by bringing her here. What do you kids think of that idea?"

Sarah smiled. "I think it will really make her way."

"Make her day, stupid."

"That's what I said."

Mary Jane held up her hand. "Wait a minute here. When we adopt a philosophy of life, it is for all of our life. We are talking about Grandma, but we are a family working together and supporting one another. Brad, what you said to Sarah did not make her day. Calling someone stupid does not make their day." Lonnie was nodding and looking seriously at Brad.

Brad looked at his feet. "I know. You should never say 'stupid.' "

"That's a good start, Brad," added Lonnie. "But the FISH! Philosophy is more than rules. When you live a philosophy, you try to live it with everyone around you. If you live it with Sarah, you are more likely to live it with Grandma. FISH! is something you can and should practice on everyone."

"Sorry, Sarah. I really don't think you are stupid. You are pretty smart for a girl."

"Brad!"

"What?"

"Think about what you just said."

"Oh. Man, this FISH! stuff is hard, Mom. Sorry, Sarah. I think you are smart. Really. I tell my friends that I have a smart sister. They tease me about it, but I am proud."

"OK, Brad. Let's not overdo it. I think you understand that it has to be genuine also."

"No, it's true, Mom. I brag about Sarah all the time. Just never when she's around."

"What you just said, Brad, is a great example of making someone's day. And if you want to know what it looks like, look at your sister."

Sarah was beaming from ear to ear.

"It is hard to stay focused, Brad, but it gets easier the

more you do it. You just have to remember that you are trying to make the world a better place to live in by the way you treat people and you are trying to make this home a better place to live by the way you treat Sarah."

"And you are trying to make your school a better place by the way you treat your classmates and your teacher," added Lonnie.

"OK, Lonnie. OK, Mom. I'll try."

Make Their Day: Sometimes you can make someone's day simply by the way you engage them.

The fish guys have an intention to engage their customers in ways that create memories, good feelings, and stories they can take with them and share after they leave. It is possible to make someone's day simply by the way you engage them, one human being to another.

- Whose day will I make today?
- How might I live my life today so as to be an inspiration to others?
- Have I treated myself to the good feelings generated by serving another?
- Am I open to having someone make my day?

BE THERE

Mary Jane glanced down at the open journal in her lap and said, "The third part of the FISH! Philosophy is Be There. This means really listening to someone and doing one thing at a time. It means not getting distracted while you are with someone. Just being there for him or her is the first step in any conversation. This will be important to Grandma and if we can do it she will know she is loved. Let me tell you kids a story about what you both did when you were babies.

Be There: Amazing things happen when you learn how to be where you actually are. Bringing consciousness, body, and spirit into the same space is a gift to yourself and to the world.

The guys at the market have mastered one of the most powerful ways to connect to other human beings, to be fully present by keeping away all distractions, quite consciously.

- Am I listening to family and friends with the single purpose of hearing what they have to say?
- Do I give the gift of rapt attention freely?

> ✎ Do we have a protocol for dealing with interruptions like the phone during a family meal?
>
> ✎ Have I reminded myself today of how good it feels to be listened to?

"I would be holding you and talking to you and someone I knew would interrupt, like in the grocery store, and I would turn my attention to them. You know what you would do? You would grab my cheeks and try to get me to look at you. You wanted me to continue to 'be there' for you. From a very young age you are aware that someone has stopped being there. It doesn't feel good when you know someone isn't there. How can we be there for Grandma?"

"She can read me stories and I can listen," said Sarah.

Brad said, "She likes it when I sit down with her rather than talking standing up."

"What do you mean, Brad?"

"Well, when we visited Grandma and she was sitting in that chair she loves, I would go in and stand by her and say hello. She would reach out and hold my hand and it was like she was holding on to me. One day I sat down and talked to her and it was different. So now I sit down, even if it is going to be a short visit. I think she likes that."

Lonnie leaned back and smiled. "You kids are great. I think you would make great fishmongers." Brad was glowing and Sarah giggled. "At the market the worst thing you can do to a customer is be distracted while you are talking to them. It ruins their market experience.

"And while we do all of these things we are going to do, what attitudes should we choose?"

CHOOSE YOUR ATTITUDE

"What is an attitude, Mom?"

"An attitude is the way you are being on the outside. We have words we use to describe how someone is being on the outside. Usually we are the same on the outside and on the inside. Sometimes we are not. We call what's on the inside 'feelings' and what is on the outside 'attitude.' We should probably discuss the difference between feelings and attitudes some time soon, but for now we will just focus on the outside, the attitudes.

"When we talk about an attitude or what we see on the outside of someone, we have words we use. We say they are happy, grouchy, positive, negative, caring, angry, bitter, patient, silly, or playful. When someone always talks about what is wrong with something, we say they have a negative attitude. When someone is like Lonnie, always seeing the good side of things and the possibilities, we say they have a positive attitude. Looking for the best in a situation is called a positive attitude. Let's talk about the attitudes we might want to choose for Grandma. What would be some good attitudes?"

"Happy," suggested Sarah.

"Patient," added Mary Jane.

"Friendly," said Brad.

"Supportive," said Mary Jane.

Choose Your Attitude: The attitude you have right now is the one you are choosing. Choose as if the quality of your life depends on it, for it actually does, moment-to-moment.

The fish guys come to work each day discussing the attitudes they are choosing. They are aware that they have the power to choose and that power enables everything else they do.

- What are the attitudes I am choosing right now?
- Do any of my current attitudes need to be replaced or will I stay with what I have?
- What attitudes do I want in my life more often?
- What attitudes do I want to avoid?
- Am I aware that feelings can't be controlled and may show up at any time without warning, but that attitudes can be chosen?
- And am I aware that sometimes the choice of an attitude can influence how I feel in the future?

Everyone looked at Lonnie, waiting for his attitude.

"Grateful. I am grateful that I am able to do something for someone who has been so important to my family. I want Grandma to see that in my attitude.

"She moved here to be closer to you kids and your mother when your father died. That was a loving and generous thing to do. I want Grandma to know I am grateful to be able to welcome her into our home. And if she decides she wants to live somewhere else, I am grateful and willing to help her accomplish that."

The family council continued to discuss attitudes for some time. The list became quite long and Sarah wanted each attitude spelled so she could write it down in large block letters.

Mary Jane looked at Sarah and thought, *Here we are talking about the FISH! Philosophy as a family and everyone is contributing. Why did it take me so long to see this possibility? Sarah is even making a list of the attitude words.*

By the end of the meeting, the family council had not only developed a list of attitudes but they had also come up with a plan for surprising Grandma and showing her by their actions how much they wanted her in their house.

An appointment would be made for Grandma at a local spa. While she was at the spa, they would move one piece of her furniture into the guest room. Then Lonnie would pick her up and the first stop would be her new room, which would be full of balloons and family; the second stop would be dinner, where they would discuss what else she would want to bring with her if she decided to stay. They would finish the day picking up essentials, and hopefully all would sleep on Queen Anne Hill that night.

"I think our attitude has become sleepy. Am I right?" asked Lonnie. Everyone smiled and the bedtime routine began.

Mary Jane reflected on the last half hour and the change in Brad. *My little boy isn't so little anymore. He seems to be carrying something heavy tonight. I need to find some time for him. No. I need to be there for him now.*

"Lonnie, I'm going to check in with Brad before I come to bed."

"You noticed too? He got quieter as the evening and the discussion progressed. Something heavy on his mind."

Mary Jane went into Brad's room. "Good night, Brad."

"Good night, Mom. That was fun."

"You got kind of quiet toward the end. Is something bothering you?"

"I was just thinking about school. You always tell me how important it is to do your best at school, but sometimes I just don't like school, Mom."

"Do you want to talk about it?"

"Mom, have you ever done something because you just want to get along?"

"Yes, I have. I know the feeling well, Brad."

"There is a kid at school who acts strange and the other kids tease him. It bothers me, but I don't do anything. And I ignore the kid even though he really hasn't done anything wrong; it's just the way he is. Talking about attitude got me thinking, that's all."

"Brad, you are thinking in a very mature and grown-up way. I am proud of you for that."

"What do you think I should do, Mom?"

"I wish I could tell you what to do but I can't. You have to decide what is right. But I can tell you there have been times in my life when doing what was right was scary because I didn't know how others might react. Maybe you can think about what we talked about tonight and see if that gives you any ideas."

"Thanks, Mom."

"Good night, Brad. I love you."

Mary Jane headed for the bathroom to get ready for bed.

"Penny for your thoughts."

"Oh, Lonnie. You startled me.

"I am thinking about how hard the life of a preteen can be. And I was thinking about the plan crafted for surprising Mom. If we had involved Mom in the discussion she would have thought and worried about nothing else until the day she moved in, if that was the decision. Now Mom will be able to avoid most of the anxiety of trying to think everything through ahead of time. I really think this a good way to approach Mom."

"Do you think she will agree to move in?"

"I hope so, Lonnie."

"Would this be a good time to have part of that conversation we agreed to have?" asked Lonnie as he sat on the edge of the old Victorian bathtub.

"Yes. I'm still wound up and awake. Talking to Brad took me back to my preteen years. Those years can be painful. Just give me a minute to take my makeup off."

There was a knock on the bathroom door, and when Lonnie opened it there stood Brad. "Sarah is crying. I think she had a bad dream."

And so the conversation was delayed, again.

The real conversations required to sustain a relationship are easily recognized.

They are the ones that keep getting put off for another day.

What Will Grandma Decide?

Three weeks had passed since the second family council, and today was the day to surprise Grandma. Mary Jane looked at her alarm clock and jumped out of bed. Pulling her bathrobe around her, she walked down the hall to rouse the kids. "Time to get up, Brad. Time to get . . ." Mary Jane opened Sarah's door only to find her on the edge of her bed fully dressed. "Sarah. How long have you been up?"

"Hi, Mom. I couldn't sleep. I was thinking about Grandma. I have a happy attitude about this, Mom."

Mary Jane sat on the bed next to Sarah and put her arm around her, with her cheek touching Sarah's. "Oh, Sarah. You are so sweet and so full of attitudes." And they just sat enjoying the moment. Then Mary Jane broke the silence.

"I'm glad you are up. I could use some help in the kitchen. Let's let Dad sleep and give Brad a second call. Why don't you call Brad and then come down to help me."

"I'm getting up. I'm getting up. Cool your jets and go away."

"Mom asked me to do this, Brad! And today is the day Grandma moves in."

"Today? Is it Saturday? I'll get up right now. Really."

When Sarah made it to the kitchen, the table was set and four boxes of cereal were already in place.

"Is your brother up?"

"He says he is getting up. I think he thought it was a school day."

"Good morning, my beautiful ladies."

"I guess I made too much noise, hon."

"I was already awake. What time do I pick up Mom and take her to the spa?"

"You should leave at eight, so I guess we can loll over breakfast for twenty-five minutes. Luxury, huh?"

Mary Jane had arranged a half-day package that included massage, hair, and nails. There was even a light lunch. This would give them four full hours to get a piece of Grandma's furniture moved from her apartment to what would hopefully be her new room on Queen Anne Hill. Two Men and a Truck, a reliable moving company, was on call if they were needed later in the day. Mary Jane handed Lonnie the schedule she had printed on a note card.

"Did you work at NASA before I met you? This is great." Brad came down with wet hair just as Lonnie was going out to the car. "Hi, big guy. See you at Grandma's house after I drop her off at the spa."

By 12:30 they had moved the headboard from Grandma's bed into the guest room, placing it in such a way that the bed location could be envisioned. Grandma's room was looking good as Lonnie headed for the door. "I love the balloons. Let's hope this works. I should be back here with Grandma in about fifty minutes. Cross your fingers."

Lonnie arrived at the reception desk of Silver Spa right on time. "I'm here to meet Mrs. Ida Gomez."

"I believe she is in the courtyard finishing lunch. I'll tell her you are here."

Lonnie was just settling in with the only available reading material, an *O, The Oprah Magazine*, when Grandma stepped into the waiting area.

Lonnie noticed her hair. "Don't you look great!"

"This was so nice of you and Mary Jane. What a treat! We even had lunch."

"Fantastic. I would like to go by the house and show you something and then I can take you home, if that is all right."

"Oh sure. Will I get a chance to see Mary Jane and the kids?"

"You bet."

"Well then, let's be on our way." And she took Lonnie's arm as they headed for the car.

Lonnie opened the front door and let Grandma go ahead and into a room full of balloons. "A party?"

"Surprise!" Mary Jane, Brad, and Sarah jumped out from their individual hiding places holding bouquets of roses with white lace.

"Surprise!"

"Surprise!"

Grandma looked a bit puzzled, as she was definitely alert enough to know it wasn't her birthday. "What? What is this all about?"

Mary Jane and Sarah each took a hand and walked her around the corner to the first-floor guest bedroom. As they entered the room the flowers were immediately placed in three vases and Grandma stared openmouthed at the headboard to her bed. "That's my headboard."

Sarah spoke up. "Grandma. We hoped you would like the way it looks in this room so much that you would want to bring the rest of your things. We would like you to live with us, Grandma."

"Oh my. You really do want me to move in with you. I always thought . . ." And Grandma lost her composure for a minute.

Sarah had been right. All she needed was to know that she was really wanted and her apartment seemed to vanish in that moment and was never mentioned again. She was now in her new home. The adjustment took about thirty seconds.

In fact, she didn't even want to make the return trip to "that old apartment," so after coffee and a pastry, everyone but Sarah and Grandma met the crew from Two Men and a Truck.

Sarah Tells Grandma About FISH!

"Do you want to see what I am doing upstairs? I have a philosophy."

"You have a what, dear?"

"A philosophy. A FISH! Philosophy."

"Oh, a philosophy? Is seven old enough to have a philosophy?"

"Oh, Grandma. Our whole family has a philosophy. Let me show you." They walked hand-in-hand up to the office.

"You can share my desk until you get one of your own, Grandma. We didn't think of that."

"I'll be fine sharing your desk, Sarah. Now tell me about this FISH! Philosophy."

"Well, Mom and Dad use it at work. It means you have fun and that part is easy for kids. You do nice things for people. You pay close attention when someone is talking and you choose your attitude. I think the attitude part is the hardest. Look at what I am doing to help me remember to choose my attitude."

Ida looked down at a desk covered with words written one at a time on round slips of paper. On one side of the desk were "happy," "positive," "loving," "helpful," "caring," "friendly," and a host of positive words. And on the other side of the desk was a smaller group that included "moody," "impatient," "angry," and "picky."

"I wrote these words down when we talked about attitude. I am making attitude badges. You take one of these attitudes and put a safety pin through it and you can wear it. Do you want me to make you one, Grandma?"

"Why of course, dear."

"Which attitude do you want to wear?"

"Do you have 'proud'?"

"I'm not sure. Do you see it? Why are you crying, Grandma? Do you want a sad one too?"

"I am not sad, Sarah. These are happy tears. I am so proud of you that I want to wear one that says that."

"Will you help me fasten the safety pin? 'Proud' will be my first complete badge."

"Sure. Hand me the material. Now what are we going to make for you?"

"Not bugging."

"Oh."

"Yes. Mom tells me that sometimes I bug Brad. I get mad when he teases me and I guess I bug him as a way of getting back at him. So I want a 'not bugging' attitude button."

"I think you will have to print another new one. I don't see it here."

"Does bugging have one or two 'g's?'"

The two of them continued working until they heard the door open downstairs.

"Hello!" Mary Jane called out.

"We're up here, Mom," responded Sarah.

"We're up here, dear," Grandma Ida called out.

Everyone assembled upstairs and Sarah took them through an explanation of the project. Brad seemed a bit skeptical about the "not bugging" button but remained pleasant. Brad chose "helpful" for himself after a great deal of thought. Lonnie chose "thoughtful" and Mary Jane decided on a pair of buttons, "here" and "now," that would reinforce her commitment to "be there." This made everyone curious, so Mary Jane explained.

"Our life is really full and we have chosen much of

what fills it to the brim. While I am going to work hard on setting better boundaries and establishing priorities, I want to be 'here now' for each moment of the life I have. I want to be fully present for each moment and stop living in the future and the past. I guess I want to bring the FISH! Philosophy to the life I have, whatever it may include."

That evening, after Grandma and the kids were settled in, Lonnie and Mary Jane were ready to carve out some time for conversation. Mary Jane said, "I'm not ready to go to bed. Do you have enough energy to talk for a while? I want to get started on our delayed conversation."

"Sure, sweetheart. But first I want to tell you how I really like the fact that you chose an attitude to reinforce 'being there.' The ingredients of the FISH! Philosophy do overlap a great deal and your choice emphasizes how you can use one ingredient to strengthen another. That is really cool.

"I think I did that at the market most of the time. There were things I didn't like and wanted to change about the market or my situation, but moment-to-moment I tried to be lighthearted and playful, bring some joy to the world, be there for other human beings, and choose my attitude wisely. The combination makes each one stronger.

"Yes, let's talk. I think we did a good thing today and I believe it was a special kind of learning experience for the children as well. I'm wide awake from the excitement of the day. Let's grab something to drink and go up to the office where we can feast our eyes on the sparkling lights of Seattle at night. I have something to ask before we get into the heavy stuff."

The Conversations Required
for a Strong Marriage

As they got comfortable, Lonnie asked, "May I bring something up that I need to get settled before we talk? I may have mentioned earlier that I have a loose end that I need to get settled, and you might remember that Jack said he had a surprise and I need to get back to Jack."

"Sure, honey."

"Well, you won't believe it. Jack has asked me to work weekends at the fish market on a part-time basis once I get settled in school and at the hospital. He says he will let me work two ten-hour days on the weekends and pay me time and a half. That's like sixty percent of my old salary and I could avoid taking out the student loan then. What do you think? I told Jack I would get back to him after I talked with you."

Mary Jane put her head in her hands and audibly moaned. Then she just held that position. The room temperature seemed to drop as the silence lengthened. Finally, Lonnie couldn't stand it any longer and asked, "Hey. What is it, honey? Did I say something wrong? Are you all right?"

With wet eyes she looked up at Lonnie. "I'm mad and angry, Lonnie, as much with myself for letting it get to this point as with you for not wanting something else. The fact that you would even consider working weekends tells me we are in two different places in this marriage. For better or worse, yes, but not parallel lives.

"I want to have a real conversation about our life together. I am angry and I want to talk about what we want and why we want it.

"What do we want in this marriage? Is the marriage just a large piggy bank into which we put as much as we can even if it means spending all of our time working? If so, to what end?"

"I can't believe you are getting so mad. I thought this was just a little thing that I could take care of before we got into the serious stuff. I guess the little thing isn't so little after all. In fact, the little thing seems to be a really big thing.

"Mary Jane, you know I've always supported myself; and growing up the way I did, I like the feeling of security that comes when I have money in my pocket and no debts. It was hard to give control of the money to you but it was the reasonable thing to do. After all, you make more and have more knowledge about finances. But it has always felt a little strange. You know, kind of unmanly. No. More like out of control.

"I thought you would be excited that I had found a way to keep from borrowing money for school and could continue making a contribution to our expenses.

"This may sound strange, but I never thought of our relationship as something we could create. I thought of us living in a world that tells us what we have to do and making the best of it. But I didn't think that way at the market so I'm not sure why I thought that here. At the market I knew we could create something extraordinary and we did.

"Look, Mary Jane, if we need to take on debt in order to have a life along the way, then I will try to swallow my fears. But I want you to understand the depth of those fears and hear me clearly. When homeless people walk through the market, I see myself in their faces. It could easily have been me. That is not an overstatement. It could easily have been me. I was that close."

Mary Jane thought deeply before she responded. "I love you, Lonnie, and I love being with you. I love the way you interact with the children. They learn so much from you. I still get a feeling of excitement when I see you walking up the sidewalk. I enjoy your intensity and sense of humor. The time we have together is precious and special. When a moment of life passes it is gone. I just want to be sure we are consciously balancing the way we spend our lives. Allocating our life energy to the things we choose, not just what comes along.

"I want great moments today and also want us to plan well for the future. I don't want to pass through this marriage saving lots of money but missing the moments, only to find that I have saved for a wealthy widowhood and

missed the marriage. It's about balance. It's about proportion and value. And it is about conversation. I don't think
the market would have maintained its energy if you guys
hadn't talked candidly with each other. Am I right?"

"We talked all the time, and we learned how to talk
about the difficult and scary things. Things like attitude
and motivation and accountability. We also talked about
skill and presentation and safety, but it was the human stuff
that made us world famous," he said.

The seeds of new growth in a relationship are planted by real conversations.

"Should I put off Washington State for a while, Mary Jane, and go back to a regular workweek? I know I can get a nurse's aide job in twenty-four hours."

"No Lonnie, that is not what I want. I was ecstatic when you were accepted at Washington State. Seeing you grow in confidence as a learner as you went through the LPN program was marvelous and exciting for me."

"Mary Jane, you asked a question earlier that got me thinking. You asked what we are building with this marriage or something like that. Well, let's talk about that. We have left too many things unsaid. You didn't know my motives for wanting to work at the market on weekends and I don't know why you are getting so involved in community activities at this time in our life together. Let's go back to the basics the way we do at the market. Let's talk about our vision for this marriage and what part we each play in bringing that vision to life. And let's do that as often as we can—starting now."

"Where do you want to start?"

"Well, let's start by talking about money, and then if we have time we can talk about sex."

"Lonnie!"

Lonnie smiled and began, "I am quite happy to say yes to home life and no to weekends at the market. I'm not sure anyone but the other guys knows how physically exhausting the work actually is. I just thought it was a necessity. Trust me. I am ready to leave the market. So let's talk about money. How are we doing? What's the deal with the outside activities?"

"I'm suddenly conscious of the fact that I have taken on all of these activities and I didn't even ask you what you thought. I have taken on the expectation of my new job that I will represent the organization in the community. I will need to do some of that, but I have a great deal of flexibility. I'm sorry for not talking to you about this."

"I appreciate that, Mary Jane, but I think your community work and weekends at the market are very different in nature. I was excited about the money, not the work. I am ready for a change. But I think representing First Guarantee in the community is about more than just money for you. I think it is about personal and professional growth. Am I right?"

"That was certainly true in the beginning, but I'm not sure now. I think I could do less and still enjoy the growth and challenge. It's more about learning how to say no to people who ask you to come talk about your success or get involved in this or that worthy cause."

"OK. There seems to have been plenty of miscommunication and blame to go around. What are we going to do now?"

"I like the idea of talking about our vision. I just wish we had a word that was less corporate. Vision, mission, goals, objectives, values, everything measurable, plan, strategy, drill down; I'm afraid the connotation for me is corporate speak."

"So what will we call it? What will we call this thing we will be using to guide our life?"

"IT."

"Yes. What will we call it?"

"IT."

"Do I hear an echo?"

"No, but it is beginning to sound like Abbott and Costello doing 'Who's on first.' "

"You want to call it IT?"

"Why not?"

"What if we committed to a lifelong conversation about our IT and the way we are living IT?"

"Sounds good to me. You start this conversation."

"OK. Our IT will contain support for the growth of each member of the family. Now you."

"We will make our choices between more money and more time together with the knowledge that we are not spending time, we are spending life. And the moments we have together are precious and valuable ways to spend life."

"We can call that the 401K clause of our IT."

"Cute."

Lonnie and Mary Jane talked late into the night and brainstormed the ingredients of their IT. They had never talked so deeply about anything and found as they talked that they had a strong desire to grow a very special relationship with each other and they were both willing to have the conversations necessary to do that. They also felt the surge of energy that comes from finally sitting down and having the difficult conversations that are the foundation of a successful relationship.

Just before they fell into each other's arms and went to

sleep Mary Jane exclaimed, "Lonnie. I'm excited. Let's keep a list of the things we want in our life together. Let's be clear about what we value and bring FISH! to those things.

"And you know we might not be able to solve all of our problems; some will take compromise or doing things that might not be our first choice. For all of those things and for each of our moments, we have our secret weapon: FISH! We can always make life better by the way we do the things we have to do anyway."

What is our vision of life together?

What are we co-creating with our life energy?

Lonnie and Mary Jane Clarify Their IT

Over the days and weeks that followed, Lonnie and Mary Jane discussed, debated, and refined their IT until they had a list of contents that they both liked.

Our IT

- We will be a couple that errs on the side of too much communication. Communication about our finances, financial priorities, and spending plans will be an area where we take the time to make sure we are clear. We will never sacrifice time together or family time for money without a discussion, and we will never assume we know what the other wants and desires.
- We will bring FISH! into our life so that even a busy schedule has an element of fun; and when we are together, we will "be there" for each other.
- We will model in our relationship the things we want our children to learn.
- We will cherish the time with Grandma Ida as a special gift and an opportunity to serve another. We will be aware of the many important life lessons our children can learn from our extended family.

- We will support each other's learning, growth, and creativity.
- We will recognize that a healthy lifestyle is always worth the effort.
- We will leave a legacy by the way we raise our children.
- Our guiding questions will be: Are we having fun? Are we serving others? Are we fully present for life's blessings, living in the now? Do our lives serve as an example of the power we all have to choose our attitude?

The 401K clause: While we understand and will teach our children the importance of planning for the future, we will emphasize the importance of living each moment fully. We will teach by example that happiness does not come from having things but from giving things to others. Happiness is not a function of the size of one's 401K, but the size of one's heart.

Contrary to popular belief,
we can't have it all.

At least not all at the same
time.

We make better choices
when those choices are
guided by our IT.

Hello, Life

It was a Monday morning and Mary Jane traveled across town to receive the results from her annual physical exam.

"Mary Jane Ramirez, come with me please. You are in Exam Room Two."

"Thank you."

She was only there a minute before Linda, her doctor, arrived to discuss the results. Linda was a physician who knew how to "be there." She had an active practice but always seemed unrushed. Mary Jane respected the fact that she always took the time to explain things and she was a great listener.

"Your tests seem fine, Mary Jane, and I think I know why you have been so tired."

"New marriage, two growing children, professional growth, late-night discussions, and a great but demanding job. I guess I might be pushing the envelope. Don't we all these days?"

"I guess we do! My youngest asked me if I could be 'on call' for him instead of everyone else. I think that was a signal.

"But I have some additional news for you that may explain why you have been feeling run down."

"I know. I have put on some weight. I really plan to do something about it, Linda."

"Well, you may want to do one additional test on your own."

"What is that, Linda, a body mass test? You call it BMI, right? I already know I am overweight."

"A pregnancy test."

"Wha . . . Wha . . . You've got to be kidding!"

"Is this bad news? Would you rather talk about your weight?"

"No. Well, I don't think so. Lonnie and I decided we would like a child together, but we would just let nature take its course. When nothing happened, we just stopped talking about it. We haven't even discussed this for over a year. It wasn't the only thing we let life crowd out of our conversations."

"Well, nature took its time and it definitely took its course."

"It's sad that one of my first thoughts was that I now have an excuse for some of the extra pounds."

"I hate to burst your bubble, but you haven't been pregnant for two years."

"Right. Thanks for the reminder."

"So, what are you going to do?"

"Wow. I don't think I'm going to work today. I want to go home and tell Lonnie before he leaves for school."

"Sounds like a plan, Mary Jane. And by the way, congratulations!"

Lonnie Gets the News

Lonnie's face was immediately enveloped by a gigantic smile and he shouted, "Wow! That's great!" Then, just as quickly as the smile came, it was replaced with seriousness. "And how do you feel about this addition to our IT?"

Mary Jane was still reacting to Lonnie's excitement. "You mean you are happy about the baby? It's another one of those things that we haven't been talking about and I wasn't sure. Are you really happy?"

Lonnie looked surprised. "How could you not know that? I don't bring it up because after we found out that we were capable of having a child I didn't want it to be a source of unnecessary pressure. Oh, Mary Jane. You didn't know?"

"I guess I didn't, Lonnie. I'm so glad we are making a more conscious effort to talk now. I feel an odd sense of direction, Lonnie, as strange as that may seem. There are certain givens in our life, the baby, Mom, the kids, and our need to keep food on the table and a roof over our heads.

"Lonnie, I think if we continue to invest time in clarifying our dreams and hopes for this marriage, it will be time well spent. I want us to continue to discuss and refine our IT. Obviously, it already needs updating.

"So go to school and enjoy every minute of the time you are there. You have been working toward this for years. What time do you think you will be home?"

"Today is the heavy schedule, so I won't see you until about 5:30."

"See you then, sweetheart. Our life changed course today."

"It did. But on a more mundane level, do you want me to pick something up for dinner?"

"No. I have a refrigerator full of leftovers and I think it may be a good idea to skip fast food for a while. Just bring yourself home. And promise we can keep the conversation alive."

Mary Jane and Lonnie did continue to keep their conversation alive. They talked every day in a way they had never talked before.

A real conversation is the
ultimate commitment to a
relationship.

A Call from Brad's Teacher

Only two weeks had passed, but now that Mary Jane knew she was pregnant the clothes seemed a lot tighter. *I should look and see if I have any maternity clothing in the attic or if I need to do some shopping. It won't be long before I will need it.*

It was Saturday and Lonnie had taken Grandma Ida and the kids to the park near the Space Needle. Grandma hauled out her photography equipment and announced she was going to teach the kids how to take good pictures. They seemed excited at the prospect but Lonnie was ecstatic. Photography was one of those things he had always wanted to do but never seemed to have time for. The phone rang.

"Hello. This is Mary Jane."

"This is Brad's teacher, Millie Johnson. I hope you don't mind my calling on Saturday. You are a hard person to reach at work."

"I'm sorry you had trouble reaching me, Ms. Johnson."

"Call me Millie. Please. And I actually prefer to call on the weekends. It avoids all the phone tag."

"We have met a couple times, but I'm sure you have trouble keeping all the parents straight."

"Actually I remember you quite well, Mary Jane. That is the way it is with the parents of kids who stand out."

"Ouch. Is Brad acting up again? I was hoping that silence meant things were better. You seemed to think he might have a learning disability."

"Oh yes. Actually I had forgotten about that. He seems to be doing well with his schoolwork. In fact, lately he always seems to have such a great attitude when he comes to school.

"But something quite extraordinary has happened. Yesterday he did the most marvelous thing."

"What exactly did he do?"

"You know we believe in mainstreaming our special students in this school system and so this year we have an autistic boy in the class. It has been a challenge. Sometimes Carr's behavior is a bit bizarre and he can't do some basic things like tying his shoes. Most kids avoid him unless I intervene and I guess that's understandable. A few make fun of him and that is unacceptable but not surprising. I have been at a loss as to what to do and it has been stressful.

"But the most amazing thing happened. Carr was walking around with his shoelaces flapping on the play-ground and Brad asked him if he could tie them for him. He did and Carr shook his hand with a smile and patted Brad on the back. It was such a beautiful moment. Later Brad asked if he could move his desk next to Carr's and he has been helping Carr ever since. They have established a kind of friendship and Carr's behavior has also changed. He is responding to the kindness and acting out less. You have one fine boy, Mary Jane, and I just wanted you to know."

"How special of you to call. You have definitely made my day. I was afraid you were calling about Brad acting out."

"Why would I be doing that?"

"Ah. Yes. Why indeed."

"And Mary Jane, I'm sorry to keep going on like this."

"Please don't be. You have made my day, Millie."

"The other children are following Brad's lead. At first a couple of them made remarks, but Brad seemed unfazed. Then the balance turned and some of the other kids started befriending Carr too. The classroom is a much better place now. Thanks again for raising such a fine boy, and have a great weekend."

"And you."

Mary Jane quickly called Lonnie to share the great news. That night she went to Brad's room and listened to her son describe how difficult it was to take the first step and how good it felt when he connected with Carr.

Other than the gift of
unconditional love, the
greatest gift you can give a
child is an understanding of
her or his power to choose.

The Weight Thing Finally Gets Attention

Lonnie and Mary Jane were having a late breakfast. Brad and Sarah had left for school an hour before and Grandma was already at the senior center located two blocks from her new home. Lonnie didn't have an early class or work at the hospital and Mary Jane responded to her morning sickness by deciding to take a personal day, so they were taking advantage of the opportunity to just be there and talk. They were living their IT.

"Mary Jane, you said something the other day that caught me off guard. Have you noticed anything different about me in the last couple of months?"

"You're better looking every day."

"Other than that."

"You have been there for me when I needed you the most."

"Thanks, honey. Have you noticed that the waist on my pants is cutting into my stomach and my belt is on the last notch?"

"No. Not really. I am very much aware of the weight I have gained, although I am relieved to learn that some of my weight gain can be ascribed to pregnancy. Maybe your body is adjusting to the loss of the high-energy fishmonger life? Your job was like an all-day aerobics class. Now you spend hours sitting in a classroom instead of being on your feet at the market."

"That could be the reason but it's new for me and I don't like it. Having a baby on the way and working with you on our IT has gotten me thinking about health. Every time we talk about our key values, health is right at the top of the list. You could say that health is at the heart of our IT. We both agree that staying as healthy as possible is something we owe each other, our children, and ourselves. It is a way to honor this wonderful life for which we are so grateful.

"So I overheard you talking with Janell about a diet she found successful. I think you used the word 'fish.' Would you mind calling her and getting the details? If she has something that works, I want to know about it—as long as it isn't too weird. Is this the fish diet where you eat nothing but salmon? I don't think I could handle all that fish after so many years staring them in the eye."

"Not that kind of fish, silly. Our kind of FISH!"

"So help me out here, Mary Jane. I don't like the feel of this belt in my gut and it seems like I'm giving up if I purchase larger clothing. I've always been on the skinny side. This is new for me."

"I will call her today and talk to her in more detail about her diet. I have been meaning to take her up on her offer to school me on her diet for my own reasons, so this will be a good time to follow up."

The FISH! Diet

Janell and Mary Jane met in the lobby of First Guarantee and walked down to Eddy's for lunch. They had each arranged things at the office so that they could take a little extra time and wouldn't have to rush through their meal.

"You started something when you mentioned that you keep your weight in a healthy range and don't just eat carrots. Not only do you have my full attention, but you have Lonnie's attention also. It seems that the life of a student has redirected some of the calories he used to burn up while on his feet at the market to his midsection.

"A solution to the battle of the bulge might be worth millions, Janell. But I would settle for maintaining a healthy weight while pregnant and losing fifteen pounds after the baby is born. So tell me. What have you got, a new secret diet? No protein, high protein, no fat, high fat, low carb, high carb, all vegetables, all fruit, ten gallons of water a day, only radishes before lunch?"

"Not to worry, Mary Jane. My plan for healthy eating doesn't focus on food."

"You see, Janell, my body mass index puts me in the obese category for the first time in my life. . . . What do you mean it doesn't focus on food?"

"Well, like I said, my ideas don't have much to do with food."

"The no-food diet. That's a novel idea! Oops. I'm getting cynical again."

"Just stay with me for a minute. What do you know about the results of most weight loss plans?"

"You lose weight and then you gain it back plus a couple pounds. After it is all over you feel like a loser but not the kind of loser you hoped for."

"That's accurate in over ninety-five percent of people who diet, Mary Jane. But let me reframe what you have just said. You said that most diets work, at least for a while. Think about it. Any given diet may not be all that healthy, but most of them work. So we all know what to do to lose weight. I believe the answer lies not in what you do—you would have to live on Mars not to know what to do. You and I probably have more knowledge about eating healthfully than we have about our college majors."

"My major was communications and it is no contest, Janell."

"I believe the solution lies in 'who you are being' while you do what you do with food. And the who you need to be is where we turn to FISH!"

"But don't you also need some diet stuff? You know, some rules."

"I do have a crib sheet of principles. It is sort of a list of some of the things we know about dieting and healthy living. I want to stay away from the extremes because you can't maintain extremes. Do you want to work with me on this and be my first student? It could be fun and I have always wanted to flesh out these thoughts more fully. This is a great opportunity!"

"Absolutely! I speak for myself and Lonnie."

Mary Jane slipped her journal out of her tote bag and began noting the wisdom of weight loss and healthy living as they brainstormed together.

Healthy Weight Control Wisdom— the Doing

1. Exercise five or six days a week for 30 minutes or more and exercise intensely for part of that time.
2. Lift weights one or two days a week.
3. Do most of the grocery shopping on the perimeter of the store where the fresh foods are kept.
4. Expect occasional slips as a part of life.
5. Always eat breakfast.
6. Eat four or five times a day and balance protein and low glycemic (sugar density) carbohydrates so as not to create highs and lows during the day. (You know what to eat.)
7. Eat nothing that is hydrogenated, avoid bad fats (you know what they are), and be sure to get the good fats like omega-3 and -6 naturally in fish or flax or in supplements.
8. Weigh yourself often and keep a chart.
9. Treat yourself once in a while with a small portion of your favorite food. This is eating healthy, not torture.
10. Find little ways to add exercise during the day, such as parking a long way from the door or using the stairs.
11. Watch carefully what food comes into the house and make tough decisions at the threshold.
12. Give the Girl Scouts money but don't take their cookies.

13. Build nonsedentary activities—such as bike-riding or walking—into the family schedule.

"That was fun. It is amazing how much we know about this subject just by being alive and aware. Every popular magazine has a monthly section on diet and health. Every morning news program has special episodes on health and diet once or twice a year. We really do already know a great deal."

"The list is just for those who want a list," added Janell. "The next part is what makes any diet effective. Since you are the one who introduced me to the most important part of my plan for weight control—a plan I have used for five years with great success—I'll let you make a guess."

"Does it have anything to do with little creatures that swim in the sea?"

"Bingo! The secret to maintaining any diet is not so much what you do but who you are being while you do what you do. And you are the expert. Give it a try and we will compare notes later. I'll leave you to your journaling now. Say hi to Lonnie. Bye."

Healthy Weight Control Wisdom— a Way of Being

"Lonnie, I talked with Janell about her weight control ideas. As I talked with her, a number of things became clear. Is this a good time to talk?"

"Are you kidding? I feel my belt digging into my stomach. Save me!"

"We live in the most weight-conscious generation in all of history. We know more about weight loss and have more special foods than any other generation. And we are the heaviest generation and getting heavier every day.

"One thing Janell and I agree on is that the most important purpose of a healthy weight control plan is not to lose weight—it is to learn how to maintain the weight you want. Quick loss and quick gain does no one any good and teaches failure. So we thought we would create a list of the wise elements of weight control and then focus on implementing and maintaining them. We all know volumes about weight loss and some of us have proven that by losing hundreds and even thousands of pounds during the course of our lives. We have to learn how to 'be' while we are dieting. We know what to do, but not how to 'be.' And that is where the FISH! Philosophy comes in. First let me show you what we brainstormed about the doing." And Mary Jane reviewed her list with Lonnie.

"I really like this 'treat yourself' part. You and Janell are right. It is amazing how much we know about weight control. So what is the FISH! Philosophy part?"

"That is up to us. We have to discover that for ourselves."

"I thought this was going to be simple?"

"It is simple. Janell says I am an expert on FISH! so you most certainly are as well. Let's do it together and start with 'play.' "

Play Keeps Life Interesting

"We could make a game out of this," said Lonnie. "We could have fun earning points, awarding prizes, and kidding around. I can see a fun scorecard on the refrigerator and the whole family participating."

"We could find some new fun ways to exercise," Mary Jane added. "I could learn how to Rollerblade so we could do it together. I have always wanted to do that."

"I have always wanted to learn how to dance. We could take one of those dancing classes at the community center. Then we could go dancing."

"Lonnie, I love to dance. I didn't think you were interested. You mean to tell me you simply don't know how?"

"Yep. I guess this plan is already paying off. And you were a communications major."

Real conversations are the
building blocks of
relationships.

Relationships are the
cornerstones of life.

"Yes, I have already been reminded of that this week. Let's continue."

"We could get one of those sleek strollers for the baby so we can fast walk or run with him."

"What do you mean 'him'?"

Lonnie smiled and shrugged. Then he suggested, "And we could approach the whole process lightheartedly, not make it too serious. Whatever we are doing we could try to make it fun!"

"Sounds like a great start. What about 'make their day'?"

Make Their Day Provides Mystery

"We can look for creative ways to support each other," started Lonnie.

"We can collect inspirational quotes and surprise each other with them."

"We can remind each other of the stakes involved and ask each other how we want to be supported."

"We can create a family savings plan and when it reaches a certain amount we could join the Queen Anne Hill Health Club."

Who are you being while you are doing what you are doing?

Be There: A Critical Success Factor

"Lonnie, I have been thinking a lot about Be There and Choose Your Attitude as they relate to healthy living. I believe that success in weight control is mostly about staying in the present moment and making good attitude choices."

"I'm not sure I know what you mean."

"Let me just focus on Be There. After I met with Janell I sat for a while and jotted a few thoughts in my journal. I began thinking about the times when I ate poorly and knew it. Here, look at my list."

**WORDS THAT DESCRIBE ME WHEN I AM
EATING POORLY AND KNOW IT:**

- emotional
- anxious
- fast
- nervous
- self-pitying
- on the run
- angry
- frustrated
- hurt
- avoiding
- medicating

"Now take anxiety as an example. Anxiety goes away if doing and being are in the same space. You feel anxious when you are in one place doing something but your mind is somewhere else. That anxiety goes away if you can be fully in the moment. That's Be There, Lonnie. It's the key."

"I see your point."

"Nervous—not present. On the run—not present. Self-pity—lives in the past and future. Frustrated—lives in the past and future.

"Do you see the pattern? The thing we call emotional eating is really unconscious eating. Emotional eating can't occur if you are being fully present. Emotion generally comes from things that have happened or things you are concerned might happen. It can only occur if you are doing the eating in the present but being in the past or the future. Once you bring doing and being together, the emotional part can't exist and you are fully conscious. Does that make sense?"

"It makes a ton of sense. We can make a discipline of being in the present and thus avoid much of life's unnecessary anxiety, at least while eating. We can create ways to become fully conscious while we eat."

"Our response to emotional cravings can be to bring ourselves into the now."

"We can be there for each other and on call 24/7 to support each other. Not as a critic but as a partner."

"What is the difference?"

"Well, a critic or a judge would say, 'Are you sure you

want to eat that?' A partner would ask, 'Are you in the present?' The energy must be natural, but we can help each other stay conscious."

"And we can talk about what we are modeling for the children and include them in our conversations about a healthy lifestyle."

"We can work at eating without television in the background and unplug the telephone. We can sit down and eat slowly with nothing other than conversation. And we can be aware that when we read the newspaper while eating we are bringing all the emotion of the world's problems to the table as well."

Choose Your Attitude:
The Source of Power

"Lonnie, I have some favorite lines from a Mary Oliver poem that I would like to represent our attitude. I have noticed when I go downstairs to use the treadmill I use the treadmill. When I put on my walking shoes and go out the front door I walk.

"These are the lines: 'One day you finally knew/ what you had to do, and began.' "

"You have nailed it, darling. It is all about taking the first step, about beginning. I heard someone say that a project started is usually finished. The hard part is taking the first step. We can choose an attitude of proactivity. We can choose to begin.

"I have another suggestion, Mary Jane. Why don't we become students of healthy living? We can take on an attitude of learning."

"I accept your amendment. Let's go for a walk. I can still do that."

"That would be fun, my dear."

"That is the point, my dear."

"Shall we begin?"

"As soon as I put on my shoes."

A FISH! diet is any *healthy* diet sustained by the natural energy of the FISH! Philosophy.

Over the next few weeks, Lonnie and Mary Jane crafted a way of living that would promote health and honor life. They worked hard to keep it simple and used what they had learned from their FISH! experiences. They agreed that a basic list of things to do was important but it was even more important to think deeply about "who they were being" while they did these things.

They kept the two lists in their office upstairs and shared reading material, ideas, and insights. Lonnie began working out at lunchtime in the university gym and he often cornered people and asked what they did, why they did it, and who they were being while they did what they were doing. These conversations became a source of new inspiration and the body of information grew.

The Maternity Ward

Lonnie and Mary Jane sat in the hospital room holding hands and waiting for five centimeters dilation.

"How ya doing?"

"I'm ready to have a baby. I should be blowing up balloons or doing something productive with all this heavy breathing."

"I'm glad you still have a sense of humor."

"Do you love me?"

"I love you."

A nurse walked in, took a look under the sheet for a minute, and said, "Let's go, folks. It's showtime." Lonnie was scrubbed and ready, so he meekly followed the entourage into the delivery room. Four hours later they were back in Mary Jane's room looking intently at the sleeping Beth Ann. They sat holding hands and thinking about how wonderful a moment can be and vowing to be present for many more of life's moments.

FISH! for Life

We all long for a primary relationship that lifts us up in a way that's not possible alone. We want to create in our lives a two that is bigger than one plus one. There is a special form of happiness that can be experienced only as two. We often think about our life partners in the following ways:

- Someone with whom to share life's little treasures: a sunset, a child's fragile first step, or a poem.
- A shoulder to cry on when life overwhelms us, and a voice to remind us of the positive futures possible in times of doubt.
- A best friend.
- Someone who knows us, warts and all, and still loves us.
- A lover with whom sex is an important part—but only a part—of intimacy.
- A ready hug.

Having someone to share one's life with may be one of the few universal longings. But meeting Mr. or Ms. Right is only a part of the equation. Happy arranged marriages expose the contradiction daily.

There is in fact some old wisdom that can strengthen any relationship and take a strong primary relationship to heights unimagined. This wisdom has been called by many names over the centuries. We call it the FISH! Philosophy and recognize that it begins, not ends, with commitment—a commitment to FISH! for Life.

Commitment comes at the beginning of a great relationship.

A FISH! for Life Discussion Guide

I have been told that the FISH! books are often used by study groups, and so with this book, I want to anticipate and welcome such a use. The following material is presented to facilitate partner, family, or reading group discussions, as well as to provide a review for the individual who wants to take the ideas deeper.

I hope this guide will help you find creative ways to put the FISH! Philosophy to work in your life. Whether you want to bring a little more fun into your family life, or find ways to serve those close to you, or make memories for grandchildren, this discussion guide has been prepared for you. Perhaps what you take away will be an understanding that life occurs in a series of moments that you are either present for or not. It might just be that the measure of a life is in part the degree to which you were present.

And if you want to transform the very foundation upon which your family or relationship is built, that is also possible.

If you are using this with your family, it is possible you will come to see that the biggest legacy you can leave your children is an understanding of the power of choice. If you are using this discussion guide with a spouse, partner, or friend, this experience will in fact be an act of relationship building.

There is no better way to feel the infinite power of integrity than in the moment we make a conscious choice of attitude. When we learn that the attitudes we have at the moment are the ones we are choosing, a door will open that is hard to close.

Of course the best way to teach any of these ingredients is to model them and discuss our choices in real conversations.

Background of the FISH! Philosophy

The FISH! Philosophy can be found in healthy and productive workplaces, homes, and relationships all over the world. For example, the FISH! Philosophy has thrived at Southwest Airlines for more than twenty-five highly successful years. They don't call it that there. It is simply their impressive culture.

The ingredients of the FISH! Philosophy were first published in the book *FISH!* They are Play, Make Their Day, Be There, and Choose Your Attitude. Documentary filmmakers from ChartHouse Learning first coined the names of these ingredients as we edited footage from the fish market.

Today these four ingredients are the standard by which

we gauge the livability of any workplace: a school, a phone center, a hospital, a bank, a plant, a fish market, or an insurance company. The right mixture assures a great place to work, even if the work itself is not all that pleasurable.

Specific FISH! Ingredient Discussion Questions

Use the following discussion questions to initiate conversation about the FISH! Philosophy. Find a question that has some energy and follow it where it takes you, remembering that the FISH! Philosophy is something that must be discovered in order to have the energy required to make a difference. The best attitudes to take into this conversation are hope, curiosity, wonderment, and openness.

PLAY: CARRY A LIGHT HEART WHEREVER YOU GO.

- How might I be an instrument of lightheartedness?
- Is there a smile in my voice?
- Do we have fun in our family? When?
- Do we value fun?
- Do we have fun as friends?
- How do we respond to someone who is always serious?
- Are we able to avoid getting too serious about

things that really don't deserve that kind of
energy?

- Do we know how to take something seriously
  while at the same time not taking ourselves too
  seriously?
- Are we using levity as a way of avoiding real
  conversations? (Play can be overdone and used
  as an escape from difficult and important
  conversations.)
- Do we see the natural joy in life?

MAKE THEIR DAY: A GREAT GIFT IS THE GIFT OF POSITIVE ENGAGEMENT.

- Whose day will I make today?
- When did someone else last make my day?
- How might the way I live my life be a source of inspiration for others?
- If my life could teach, what would the first lesson be?
- What memories did I create for my children today?
- How will I make someone's day brighter today?
- Who goes unnoticed in my world?
- Is there a way to bring special attention to those who toil in the background of my life? (The people who greatly affect the quality of our lives by keeping the floors clean, the streets safe, and the food on the shelves could use a kind word once in a while.)
- What am I doing to make the world a better place?
- What do my children and grandchildren remember about their time with me? (You never know when you are making a memory. You can know when you are being FISH!)

BE THERE: AMAZING THINGS CAN HAPPEN WHEN YOU LEARN TO BE WHERE YOU ARE.

- Where am I right now? Where is my attention? What are the currents wandering through my mind?
- Are my mind and body in the same place?
- Where do I want my attention?
- What is the impact of my "be there" decision?
- Am I one place at a time, doing one thing at a time, or do I try to do many things at once?
- Is it true that even if I multitask I can still do only one thing at a time?
- Do people know when my attention is somewhere else?
- What do I think of Brad's discovery about sitting down with Grandma rather than talking to her standing up? Have I ever experienced the same sort of thing?
- What cues can we give one another to promote the now?

CHOOSE YOUR ATTITUDE: THE ATTITUDE YOU HAVE RIGHT NOW IS THE ONE YOU ARE CHOOSING. CHOOSE WISELY, FOR YOUR LIFE DEPENDS ON IT.

- What attitude(s) are my favorites?

1.

2.

3.

- What attitudes are most common in my life?

1.

2.

3.

- Do I like those attitudes?
- How do I shift from one attitude to another?
- Do I have a system to remind me to do frequent attitude checks?
- Are there quick ways to assume an attitude?
- Do I have a default attitude?
- Do I separate feelings and attitudes?
- What are some ways to get out of an attitude?
- What attitudes in others are like fingernails on a blackboard?

General Discussion Questions

The following are some general questions that can be used to initiate important conversations with those you love. They are meant to provide possibilities from which to choose, rather than to be discussed in any particular order. You might simply use them to provoke your own important questions. Remember that these conversations need to be both real and fierce. This is not just talk or chitchat. These are the conversations that build a relationship with their courage, compassion, and candor. Commit to having one real conversation a week with the people who are most important to you.

What does it mean for us to have a conversation that is real and fierce?

Are there subjects we have been avoiding?

What is our vision for this family, partnership, or friendship?

Do we understand our IT?

Is it serving us well?

What are we creating with our life together?

How can we help each other stay in the present?

What attitudes would we like to have present in our life together and what are some ways we can make that happen?

What are the seven basic values that sit at the heart of the life we are building together?

➤ List them:

1.

2.

3.

4.

5.

6.

7.

➤ Inventory their presence and proportion in your life.

➤ Does their presence and proportion match your sense of appropriate balance? Would you like to see more or less emphasis on any of these values?

➤ Discuss goals for the next year/six months/day.

➤ Review.

Commitments

This page is blank. It is up to you to fill it. So why not slowly fill it with commitments. What are you willing to commit to and with whom? Write it down. Come back here often. Your life is at stake.

The wisdom contained in the FISH! Philosophy can also be found in each of us.

You have everything you need to begin.

Go FISH! for life.

We would like *your* participation in *The FISH! for Life Companion*

Send us your stories and become a part of *The FISH! for Life Companion*. The following are four examples of the stories that have been sent to us over the last three years by women and men who have taken FISH! home. Send us your FISH! story if you would like your story to be a part of *The FISH! for Life Companion*.

PLAY
From an email received anonymously:

One night after dinner my parents sat upside down in their chairs with their feet sticking up the back of the chairs and their heads hanging upside down under the table. Of course, my sister and I joined them, and we laughed until our stomachs hurt. It's one of my favorite memories of growing up.

MAKE THEIR DAY
What I love about this idea that came in an email is that it takes a normally negative situation and uses "make their day" to create a positive. If you recognize this story, please contact me so I can give you credit. You are a fabulous storyteller.

Good behavior comes from good preparation. I learned this lesson from my daughter's first visit to the dentist. We were prepared for the second visit.

While staying at my parents' one weekend, I realized how much their La-Z-Boy and swivel reading light resembled a dentist's chair. With my daughter as my assistant, we assembled a tray complete with Gram's toothbrush, toothpaste, dental floss, and a Dixie cup of water. We asked Gram to lie back, positioned the light, and placed a napkin under her chin. My dad stood over our shoulders dramatically making the sound of a dentist's drill. (I must say he enjoyed playing his part.) We were quite proud of our work: Gram came out of it with relatively clean teeth and very little bleeding. "Dentist" has now become a favorite game for my daughter and her cousins to play at Gram and Papa's. None of us has had a cavity since.

BE THERE

From a phone call:

I had been telling my boys for some time that I would go camping with them in the backyard. They were very excited about sleeping in a tent. Considerable time passed and there was always some reason to put it off until the following week. The boys stopped asking when it would happen and I must admit I was relieved. Then I read about "be there" and the dedication you made to your daughter who was killed by a drunk driver. The next morning I looked in the mirror and made a commitment to "be there" for my sons and to be a part of their lives. We had a ball sleeping outside last night.

CHOOSE YOUR ATTITUDE

From an email:

If you have a morning when you know you will be in a hurry or if you have a toddler who hates getting dressed in the morning, what's the crime in letting her sleep in her clean clothes for the next day? So what if the rest of the world chooses pajamas at night. If it makes it easier for the family to choose a happy attitude the next morning, then do it. **Caution:** Don't tell your mother about this, as grandmas don't understand these kinds of things.

SLRunner@aol.com is the email address to use when you send in your ideas for the *FISH! for Life Companion*. It is my hope that we have a book full of stories from everyday people using the FISH! Philosophy to improve their lives, strengthen their relationships, and raise their children. All contributions will not necessarily be published, but by sending us your story you are giving us permission to print it and to do any necessary editing.

Thanks for making *FISH! for Life*.

Stephen C. Lundin
Big Tuna Ph.D.

Acknowledgments

We would like to first acknowledge our families. Harry would like to thank Mary, his wife, and Rachel and David, his children, for the joy they bring him and the unwavering support they have provided as he has taken FISH! on the road.

John would like to recognize his wife, Gaye, and his daughters, Tori and Kelsey. They have been the constants in his life as he has dealt with the challenges of providing leadership to his company, ChartHouse.

And I would like to thank my wife, Janell, for her support, love, and wisdom. She is the first person who reads what I write and her comments are always spot on. My daughters Beth, Melissa, and Melanie are no longer under the same roof with us, but I feel their presence daily—and their enthusiasm, love, and support have been brilliant. And speaking of brilliant, my high-tech son-in-law Paul keeps me on my toes by reminding me what it means to live a full, creative, loving, and productive life.

All I can say about our publisher, Hyperion, is "Wow!" This is the fourth time I have acknowledged their contribution and each time I feel more gratitude and respect for the amazing work they do. The great folks we work with at Hyperion are Bob Miller, Ellen Archer, Jane Comins, Mark Chait, Kiera Hepford, Corinna Harmon, Jill Sansone, Sharon Kitter, Mike Rentas, and Adrian James. They are all magnificent, but the guy I want to single out for special recognition is the extraordinary Will Schwalbe. Will, your patient guidance, wise insights, enthusiasm, and thoughtfulness are cherished. You set the standard, Will, and there is so much I have learned under your guidance. I consider my time with you precious.

One of our great decisions was to choose Margret McBride as an agent. She has been and still is remarkable. We are aware that during the last year she has felt the very pressures we write about in this book as her aging parents consumed large amounts of her time and energy. Our respect for her only grew as she gracefully dealt with some of life's biggest challenges. We want to express our appreciation to you, Margret, for your fabulous contributions and to also send our love and support to you in these difficult times. The staff at McBride Literary Agency includes Donna DeGutis, Renee Vincent, Faye Atchison, and Anne Bomke.

Bring the FISH! Philosophy deeper into your organization

ChartHouse Learning has created a family of amazing resources to help you bring the many benefits of the FISH! Philosophy into your life at work. These resources include the award-winning films FISH!, FISH! STICKS, and FISH! TALES as well as books, live learning presentations and FISHin' Gear. To learn more, visit us at:

www.fishphilosophy.com

Have you been inspired by the FISH! Philosophy at work, school or home? Are you doing anything differently because of the FISH! Philosophy? If you have a story you would like to share, contact us at:

fishtales@charthouse.com

At ChartHouse Learning, our goal is to inspire people to an awareness that transforms their experience of work and life into one of deep aliveness and purpose. For more about ChartHouse learning programs, visit:

www.charthouse.com

CHARTHOUSE
LEARNING

1-800-328-3789

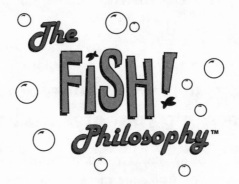

Our Speakers:
FISH!™ Philosophers & Storytellers.
Guides for the Journey Ahead.

We are ready to help you bring The FISH! Philosophy to life wherever you are! ChartHouse Learning has speakers and facilitators who travel the globe spreading The FISH! Philosophy to those who are searching for a better way to live at work, school and home.

For more information about live events, speeches, teacher training or curriculum designed for the classroom and the boardroom, please contact our Live Learning department at **1-800-328-3789** or visit **www.fishphilosophy.com.** For information on booking Harry Paul as a speaker contact: thepauls@cox.net.

To contact the authors, email them at:

Steve Lundin:
steve@charthouse.com

John Christensen:
john@charthouse.com

Harry Paul:
thepauls@cox.net

NOTES